ANIMALS IN THE GREAT WAR

ANIMALS IN
THE GREAT WAR

STEPHEN WYNN AND TANYA WYNN

Pen & Sword
MILITARY

AN IMPRINT OF PEN & SWORD BOOKS LTD.
YORKSHIRE - PHILADELPHIA

First published in Great Britain in 2019 by
PEN AND SWORD MILITARY
An imprint of
Pen & Sword Books Ltd
Yorkshire – Philadelphia

ISBN 978 1 47383 804 8

Typeset in Times New Roman 11.5/14 by
Aura Technology and Software Services, India
Printed and bound in England by TJ International,
Padstow, Cornwall, PL28 8RW

Pen & Sword Books Limited incorporates the imprints of Atlas, Archaeology,
Aviation, Discovery, Family History, Fiction, History, Maritime, Military, Military
Classics, Politics, Select, Transport, True Crime, Air World, Frontline Publishing,
Leo Cooper, Remember When, Seaforth Publishing, The Praetorian Press,
Wharncliffe Local History, Wharncliffe Transport, Wharncliffe True Crime and
White Owl.

For a complete list of Pen & Sword titles please contact
PEN & SWORD BOOKS LIMITED
47 Church Street, Barnsley, South Yorkshire, S70 2AS, England
E-mail: enquiries@pen-and-sword.co.uk
Website: www.pen-and-sword.co.uk

Or
PEN AND SWORD BOOKS
1950 Lawrence Rd, Havertown, PA 19083, USA
E-mail: Uspen-and-sword@casematepublishers.com
Website: www.penandswordbooks.com

Contents

Foreword

Seeing as this is a book on animals, we are going to be somewhat self-indulgent and mention the three cats, eight guinea-pigs and nine dogs that have been companions throughout the course of our lives.

Special mention goes to one of our German Shepherds, Dexter. When we began writing this book, he was already undergoing chemotherapy for blood cancer after having had his spleen removed. As a result of the operation and four sessions of chemotherapy, he had twelve weeks of additional, quality life, which provided us with many great memories. He had a sudden relapse, and sadly passed away at 8.30am on Tuesday, 17 July 2018. His passing was painful, but he will remain in our hearts and memories forever more.

Dexter.

Introduction

Animals and war have gone hand in hand for thousands of years. The earliest evidence of horses being used in warfare dates back to Eurasia, sometime between 4000 and 3000 BC. The years between 1600 and 1350 BC saw the use of horse drawn chariots throughout the area which roughly covers what is known as the Middle East today.

The earliest use of saddles on horses, or what then passed for saddles, can be traced to around 700 BC by Assyrian cavalry.

In about 360 BC, the skills required to be able to ride a horse in combat were written about by a Greek cavalry officer, by the name of Xenophon.

The story of the Carthaginian Hannibal's epic crossing of the Pyrenees and the Alps in the year 218 BC, with men, horses and elephants, on his way to fight the Romans during the Second Punic War, has been told and retold a thousand times. People still marvel at his sheer temerity at even having considered doing what he did.

The middle of the nineteenth century saw the Charge of the Light Brigade, which took place at Balaklava on 25 October 1854, during the Crimean War. The charge, which was part of the Siege of Sevastopol, was led by Lord Cardigan against Russian forces, when just over 600 troopers of the Light Brigade charged into the valley between the Fedyukhin Heights and the Causeway Heights. By the end of the charge, 110 of the troopers had been killed, with a further 161 wounded.

By the First World War, cavalry were almost obsolete and probably would have been entirely, if it hadn't been for the large number of senior officers who had started out as cavalry officers in the initial years of their military service. There were many cavalry charges during the First World War, there was even one on the very last day of the war at Levinnes in Belgium, though the reason why is not at all clear. One of the most notable cavalry charges took place two weeks into the Battle of the Somme, on 14 July 1916, on the outskirts of the village of Bazentin le Petit.

An area known to the British as High Wood and to the Germans as the *Bois des Fourreaux*, was fought over by British and German forces over the course of 14 and 15 July. Its name has changed slightly, and is today known as the *Bois des Fourcaux*.

There were many different types of animals used in the First World War, horses certainly weren't the only ones that were used. Donkeys and asses were used to convey artillery pieces, ammunition and other equipment to and from the front line. Dogs, cats and pigeons were employed for different military purposes, and others, such as a springbok of the 4th South African Regiment, were used as mascots.

Chapter 1

Pigeons

The homing pigeon is a domestic bird found all across the United Kingdom, with the ability to travel extremely long distances to find its way back home. It is able to do this by using magnetoreception, which according to Wikipedia is:

> A sense which allows an organism to detect a magnetic field to perceive direction, altitude or location. This sensory modality is used by a range of animals for orientation and navigation, and as a method for animals to develop regional maps, for the purpose of navigation.

Soldiers preparing to release messenger pigeon.

Over the relatively short distance for a pigeon of say, 400 miles, they could quite comfortably maintain a good average speed in the vicinity of 50 miles per hour.

Unlike humans, who have front-facing eyes, pigeons have monocular vision, which means they have to move their heads each time they take a step, to be able to maintain their depth of perception. In essence, a pigeon can see and focus on something that is a static, rather than a moving object.

The use of pigeons as messengers can be traced back to Persia and Syria in around the 5th century BC. Over the following centuries the practice of sending messages by pigeon between towns and cities, as a means of communication, was developed all over the area which is today known as the Middle East. It was like an early postal system. The Romans were another civilisation who used pigeons to communicate with different realms of their Empire.

News of the outcome of the Battle of Waterloo was first received back in England by means of a messenger pigeon, so widespread was their use as a way of communication.

Over 100,000 pigeons were used as military messengers by the British Army during the First World War, often carrying vital information from

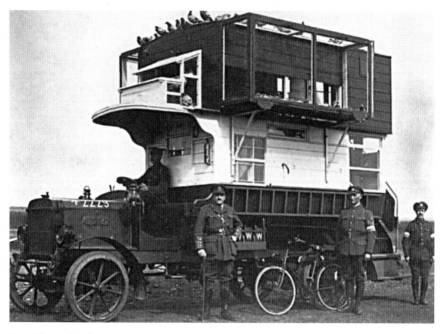

Bus Pigeon Loft.

the front line trenches to brigade headquarters; a dangerous role, even for a pigeon. But despite the danger, their success rate at delivering their messages was extremely high.

They were possibly more widely used than was actually appreciated. Most people think of them flying about in the trenches on the Western Front, sending vital messages all over the place, which they did, but they were also used from on board ships. If a vessel of the British Royal Navy was in a battle on the high seas, the chances were that the ship's radio operator would have sufficient time to get off a message, but if they suffered a surprise attack by a German submarine, the only option for the crew of a quickly sinking ship might have been to send a messenger pigeon. Armed with the details of their last position at the time of their sinking, a pigeon might mean the difference between life and death for any crew.

One of the ways in which troops on the front line could communicate with their headquarters was by sending messages attached to a pigeon's leg. To accommodate this facility, mobile pigeon lofts were erected immediately behind the front line trenches, to allow messages to be sent expediently. The lofts were either transported on the back of horse-drawn lorries or mounted on mechanically propelled vehicles such as modified ambulances or London buses. When needed, the birds would be gathered from the lofts, before being taken to the forward trenches in small wicker baskets in readiness for release.

Pigeons with what look like cameras strapped to their chests.

By the very nature of the circumstances involved, it was always going to be somewhat hit and miss. On most occasions a pigeon was only sent in a dire emergency in the heat of battle, which meant that the environment in which they had to fly wasn't necessarily conducive to their health or wellbeing. Once released they would have to contend with having to fly through poisonous gas and artillery bombardments, meaning their survival was often dependent on their speed and agility. A pigeon was released for different reasons. It might be sent with a request for reinforcements, an artillery bombardment, food or ammunition, but there were also times when it was sent with intelligence information concerning German troop movements or positions, important for those back at headquarters planning future Allied attacks to be aware of.

Sending messages by pigeon was a one-way trip, as they were only trained to fly back to a location they already knew, which meant that once they had delivered their message, they couldn't then fly back to the place they had been released from. They would then require to be transported to wherever they were next needed, which wasn't always where they had been previously sent from. But no matter where they were transported to, once released, they would always return to the same location, the place they knew as 'home'.

The Germans became somewhat crafty when it came to dealing with the threat posed to them by the release of pigeons. Initially, every time the British released one, the Germans knew this meant that some kind of message was being sent, so they would immediately respond with a barrage of rifle and machine-gun fire, in an attempt to bring the bird down. Not satisfied with this, they later responded by bringing trained hawks up to their front lines and releasing them after the pigeons.

Throughout the United Kingdom, restrictions on the keeping of pigeons were governed by the regulations under the Defence of the Realm Act 1914. As a result of this there were numerous occasions of individuals being prosecuted and put before the courts.

At the Bedford Petty Sessions on Wednesday, 12 May 1915, Mr Wilhelm Kitchiner of Biggleswade, was charged with shooting a tame pigeon in the town on 23 April 1915.

Mr Montague Austin, the solicitor representing the National Homing Union, told the court that although on the face of it the shooting of a pigeon, which had been valued at the sum of 5 shillings, appeared somewhat of a small matter, because of the present circumstances in which the country found itself, this was in fact a serious situation. Shooting any kind of pigeon, for whatever reason, was potentially serious for those involved, as they might be shooting a pigeon that was carrying a message, as it wasn't only in foreign war zones that the British authorities were using the birds for official purposes.

The circumstances in this case were as follows. Police Constable Jones was standing on the Ivy Bridge, which overlooked Mr Moffat's nursery, when a flight of pigeons went up. As they flew overhead, Mr Kitchener fired towards the flock of birds, killing one of them in the process. As the bird hit the ground, a small boy picked it up, and Mr Kitchiner shouted to him to put it under his coat.

The magistrates' clerk enquired as to whether it was a carrier pigeon. Mr Austin confirmed that it was just an ordinary pigeon, but was one of a number that belonged to Mr Day of the Ongley Arms Inn.

Mr Kitchiner told the court that he saw two birds which he believed to be pigeons, but one of them turned out to be a jackdaw. He was about 80 yards away when he opened fire, hitting the bird. He believed that it was a wild bird.

Police Superintendent Nicholson told the court that he had heard of numerous similar other incidents of pigeons being shot, before and since the war had begun. His assumption on the matter was that due to food shortages, people saw pigeons as an alternative food source, and when the chance arose to put some extra meat on the table, certain individuals were more than willing to seize the opportunity.

Mr Kitchiner informed the court that as soon as he realised that he had in fact shot a pigeon, he reported the matter to the police. The Chairman of the Bench determined that the matter would be dealt with by way of a fine of 10 shillings, but reiterated that the shooting of any kind of pigeon whilst the war was on was a very serious matter.

On Monday, 23 August 1915, Frederick William Park of 479 Bolton Road, Stubshaw Cross, was summonsed to appear at Wigan County Police Court, for keeping and carrying homing pigeons short distances without a permit. He pleaded guilty, but in mitigation stated that he didn't know that he was doing any harm.

The magistrates' clerk, Mr A. Smith, asked Park: 'Have you kept pigeons before?'

Park: 'No sir.'

In answer to further questions by the magistrates' clerk, Park stated that he had never flown the pigeons before nor taken them away. He had owned the pigeons for about a month, during which time they had not even been out on the roof of his house.

Having listened to what Park had said, the summons for carrying the birds was withdrawn, and a fine of 5s 6d was imposed. The Chairman of the Bench, Mr S. Walsh, JP, said that as this was the first case of its kind that had been brought before them, they were inclined to take a rather lenient view of the matter, and were happy to deal with it by way of the fine imposed. He hoped word of this case would be widely reported so that the message was heard by others, loud and clear, that it was an offence to keep or carry homing pigeons without a permit.

Mr Thomas Tunstall of 278 Bolton Road, Stubshaw Cross, Wigan, the same street as Mr Park, was summonsed for keeping ten homing pigeons without a permit. He pleaded guilty, and stated that he didn't know that he needed a permit for the pigeons. He had never flown the pigeons, and that Police Constable Johnson had called at his home and informed his wife that if the birds didn't fly, he didn't need a permit for them. Police Constable Johnson gave evidence which supported what Tunstall had said, stating that he had told him this on 21 April 1915, but since that date the notices in relation to the keeping of pigeons had changed in line with a further order issued by the War Office, and that this new order had been circulated and publicised.

Mr Walsh asked Police Constable Johnson if he had personally informed Mr Tunstall of these changes, and he replied that he had not. As with Mr Park, the magistrates imposed a fine of 5s 6d.

Mr William Tunstall, of the same address, had also been summonsed for the offence of keeping and carrying homing pigeons without a permit. He pleaded guilty, and was also fined a similar sum of money.

One of the most famous war-time pigeons was named *Cher Ami*, who, on one occasion was shot en route to his destination, but still managed to find his way home, and in doing so helped saved the lives of some 200 men from the nine companies of the United States 77th Infantry Division's 'Lost Battalion'.

This came about after an American attack on German defensive positions in the Argonne Forest, during the Meuse-Argonne Offensive, which took place between 26 September and the signing of the Armistice on 11 November 1918. Out of a starting number of 554 officers and men, about 196 were subsequently killed in action, with 164 either missing in action or taken prisoner of war, whilst the remaining 194 were rescued alive.

Their commanding officer, Major Charles White Whittlesey, led his men of the 77th in an attack into the Argonne on 2 October 1918. He did this under the belief that elements of the French Army were supporting their left flank, and two units of the 92nd Infantry Division were supporting them on the right. The units under Whittlesey's command quickly made significant headway against the German defenders in their path. What Whittlesey didn't know, and hadn't been informed of, was both the French and American units supporting their flanks had stalled. This quickly resulted in Whittlesey and his men being surrounded by German forces. The following six days would see some ferocious fighting between the men of the 'Lost Battalions', the Germans who had surrounded them and the men of the United States 92nd Infantry Division, who were attempting to relieve them.

Despite the casualties they sustained, the men of the 77th also suffered many hardships. They were low on food, and to collect water they had to crawl to a nearby stream, usually whilst under fire. As time passed, ammunition became less and less and all of the 'runners' who Whittlesey sent out were either killed, captured or got lost. The last resort to try and make contact with their headquarters was the unit's carrier pigeons. In an unfortunate incident on 4 October 1918, incorrect coordinates that had been recorded and attached to a pigeon's leg resulted in a friendly fire incident. Not to be defeated, men of the US Army Signal Corps, who were serving alongside Whittlesey's men, sent *Cher Ami* into the affray. She was a homing pigeon who had been donated to the US Army, by the Pigeon Fanciers of Great Britain. She carried the following message:

> We are along the road paralell 276.4. Our artillery is dropping a barrage directly on us. For heavens sake, stop it. [*sic*]

Despite being badly wounded the bird survived and was sent back to the United States, but died a year later. It was only after *Cher Ami* had passed away that it was discovered that she was a hen and not as she

Pigeon Cher Ami.

had first been registered, a cock. Her stuffed remains, and her wooden leg, are on display at the Smithsonian Institution in Washington DC.

Whittlesey's men managed to hold on until they were rescued by other Allied units who had broken through the German lines, forcing them to retreat. The fact that Whittlesey's men were able to hang on, was a testament to the bravery and steely determination of *Cher Ami*. She was awarded the French Croix de Guerre for her heroic war time service.

Pigeon Service Manual

(1) Unless one has been intimately in touch with pigeons at one of the active Air Stations where a Pigeon Service has been established, their usefulness and value is not appreciated. That their 'Service rendered' has been of inestimable value there is no doubt, and pilots and observers are to be found everywhere who owe the saving of their lives to the agency of these little winged heroes. Heroes they are, for on occasions they have fought their way through the most adverse weather conditions carrying messages which meant everything to those liberated by them.

(2) It has therefore become necessary to issue a publication explaining to some extent their capabilities, management and use, in so far as required by the Royal Air Force, for the guidance of all concerned. This manual, therefore, is only intended to supply information applicable specially to the use of pigeons from aircraft, and not contained in the ordinary text books on the subject of pigeons.

(3) The pigeon used today for message service has been bred for generations from selected parents, all of whom have established their merits by homing from distances, in some cases as great as 500 or 600 miles.

(4) In order to obtain the best possible results from pigeons employed by the Royal Air Force, pigeon experts with a thorough knowledge of the training and care of pigeons are placed in charge of the lofts. This is an assurance to pilots that only reliable pigeons are supplied to them.

(5) Pilots and observers should be thoroughly conversant with the handling of pigeons, and for this purpose instructional lofts have been erected.

(6) Experience has shown that pigeons to be used from aircraft require a special education for this class of work.

(7) Although the Pigeon Service personnel is composed of experts, the training of pigeons from aircraft varies considerably. Therefore, each man on entering the Service is given a course of instruction at one of the established centres in the management and maintenance of an RAF pigeon loft.

(8) It has to be borne in mind that owing to the vagaries of the weather, the difference in the condition of the birds themselves and again, the varying results obtained according to the season of the year, the Pigeon Service generally is not intended to take the place of any existing means of communication, but to serve as an auxiliary.

(9) The success of the Service depends largely on cordial and unselfish cooperation. Unless officers commanding units arrange that all necessary facilities for the training of birds are provided for the expert, the pigeon will not be fit for the work it is called upon to do. As a rule, pigeons are not used until all other means of communication fail. Therefore, their messages in many cases hold the balance between life and death.

Under the Defence of the Realm Act 1914, Regulation 21, it was an offence to 'kill, wound, or molest' homing pigeons, although it is not quite clear what actually constituted the molesting of a pigeon. For committing such an offence a person could be sentenced to six months' imprisonment, or a fine of £100, which would be somewhere in the region of £3,200 today. The poster reminded members of the public that 'Homing Pigeons' were doing valuable work for the government, and that they were requested to 'assist in the suppression of the shooting

DEFENCE OF THE REALM
Regulation 21A.

SHOOTING
HOMING PIGEONS.

Killing, Wounding or Molesting Homing Pigeons

is punishable under the Defence of the Realm Regulations by

SIX MONTHS IMPRISONMENT OR £100 FINE.

The Public are reminded that Homing Pigeons are doing valuable work for the Government, and are requested to assist in the suppression of the shooting of these birds.

£5 REWARD

will be paid by the NATIONAL HOMING UNION for information leading to the conviction of any person SHOOTING HOMING PIGEONS the property of its Members.

Information should be given to the Police, Military Post, or to the Secretary of the Union, C. C. PLACKETT, 14. EAST PARADE, LEEDS.

Poster about the killing of pigeons.

of these birds'. The country was, after all, experiencing the effects of rationing, so the opportunity to shoot a few pigeons was one way of guaranteeing meat on the table for tea.

The poster also pointed out that the National Homing Union would pay a £5 reward for information leading to the conviction of any person for the shooting of Homing Pigeons.

Chapter 2

Elephants

Soldiers of the Indian Royal Field Artillery didn't use horses to move about the artillery pieces of their heavy batteries. Instead they used elephants. Each of these sagacious creatures weighed several tons. They might not have been able to move as quickly as thoroughbred horses, but they could pull and haul heavy artillery pieces all day long, with no help from anybody.

Elephants could go places that no mechanised vehicle could reach, and just one of them was able to easily do the work that would usually take four or six horses to do.

Before the start of the First World War, the Indian Army was equipped with a number of heavy artillery batteries, and to move their large

Indian elephants pulling an artillery piece.

howitzer artillery pieces around they used the country's favourite heavy animal, the elephant. Although one was more than capable of hauling the gun, the carriage and the crew, it was usual for two elephants to be allocated to each carriage, that way if it became bogged down in heavy mud, the lead elephant could be unhooked and sent round to the rear of the carriage to use his massive head and 8 ton of weight to add support by pushing.

There was a fine balance to be struck when it came to the use of the elephants anywhere near the fighting line, which is where they needed to be, but if they got too close they were a very big target for the enemy, almost too big to be able to miss. The relationship that each of them had with their individual handlers made for a constructive interaction, as when trained to a sufficient standard, they could be quite disciplined beasts.

Each of the elephants had its own official record. The information recorded on it included the elephant's age, its length of service, and even information about its character, the latter of which was more important than it might at first appear. If an elephant was prone to being temperamental, its suitability to carrying out such work might be questionable. If an elephant did misbehave it wasn't unusual for it to be left chained up by one of its legs and reduced of its treats. Those who behaved received their usual treats of sugar, cakes and apples. It was a sight to behold to see elephants willingly working, carrying out parade, drill and marching, keeping rank, and even keeping themselves clean. It was even said a sign of their happiness was shown when they saluted by raising and lowering their trunk.

One thing which could negatively affect an elephant's behaviour quite badly was toothache, or rather tusk ache. If debilitated by disease, a tusk could be entirely hollowed out or eaten away. Elephants actually have extremely sensitive nerves, so a decaying tusk could literally send them mad. Those who have experience of them in captivity say that toothache can affect elephants in a more severe manner than it does any other animal, and it is one of the more frequent causes of why they suddenly run amok. Not surprising when considering the length of an average elephant's tusk.

Elephants were domesticated by the ancient Carthaginian civilisation who deployed them in their wars with Rome, a struggle that was finally won by the Romans in 146 BC, with the fall of Carthage, in what is today Tunisia, on the north-east coast of Africa.

Seleucid Coin (Harmann Linge)

The historian of the Maccabees tells us that the Army of Artischus allocated 1,000 men, wearing coats of chain mail, and some 500 horsemen, to accompany every elephant into battle. The Maccabees were a group of Jewish rebel warriors who took control of Judea, part of the Seleucid Empire which existed from 312 BC to 63 BC. Their coinage included images of both horses and elephants.

In mobilising elephants from Hagenbeck's zoo and employing them to clear the roads around Valenciennes in the First World War, the German military authorities once more reverted to these same long ago ancient ways.

Many authorities on the matter maintain that Julius Caesar brought elephants to Britain and used them for military purposes during the second invasion of 54 BC. Part of an entry on Wikipedia reads as follows:

> By the time Caesar reached the Thames, the one fordable place available to him had been fortified with sharpened stakes, both on the shore and under the water, and the far bank was defended. Second century sources state that Caesar used a large war elephant, which was equipped with armour and carried archers and slingers in its tower, to put the defenders to fight. When this unknown creature entered the river, the Britons and their horses fled and the Roman army crossed over and entered Cassivellanus' territory.

The topic of the use of elephants in the war was often an issue that was at odds with itself. It seemed to be that throughout Europe, on the

Allies side as well as the Germans, they were appreciated as a much-needed presence and resource for doing heavy work on the home front in connection with each side's war effort. They were also used for direct military purposes by certain Indian Regiments. Because of the large number of horses that were 'commandeered' for the military, the use of elephants became less of a shock.

Compare this if you will with the report in June 1915, of the 'celebrated' elephant hunter, Mr James Sutherland, who hailed from Leith in Scotland but had left for the African shores in 1895, where in turn he became a miner, an actor, and a pugilist (professional boxer). He had also become an author in 1913, when he had a book published, in which he wrote about his 'adventures' as an elephant hunter. He later became a guide and an adviser to the British Army stationed in Nyasaland. On one occasion he reportedly made an enforced march of 500 miles in twenty-three days to escape being captured and taken prisoner by the Germans. He had been wounded whilst in Nyasaland, whether by an elephant or a German bullet wasn't clear, but it was deemed to be sufficiently newsworthy to report the matter in the press. Despite being much needed and greatly relied on back home, it was OK to slaughter them at will because there was an abundance of them in Africa. Those who made a good living out of killing them by selling their tusks were somehow seen as 'bloody nice chaps' who were brave fellows and full of derring do.

In July 1915, an 'elephant' and the military, once again were partnered with one another, but on this occasion the coupling of the two was somewhat of an unusual one.

An almost entire fossil elephant of an enormous size was excavated in the grounds of the Royal School of Military Engineering at Upnor, near Chatham, Kent. The elephant in question belonged to the species known as *Elephas antiquus*, which walked the earth in the early Pleistocene epoch time, and was even larger than a mammoth, which in turn was far bigger than an elephant of today.

It is believed to have been common to the area where it was found, and an animal which enjoyed milder temperatures than the hot climates where today's elephants originate from. From other examples of this elephant that had been discovered in the frozen tundra of Northern Siberia, they were covered in a coat of shaggy red hair.

In July 1915, a strange case came before the County Court in Birmingham. Major Charlton Watson Spink, who was serving with the

Royal Field Artillery, had before the outbreak of the First World War, worked as the Resident Administrator in Amadi, Mongallo, in Central Africa. In August 1913, Major Spink was back in London on leave, and was preparing to return to his work in Mongallo when he called upon a firm to whom he had been in the habit of giving a yearly order for ammunition. The ammunition in question was for eighty rounds of 470 solid rifle cartridges for tropical charges, which was sent to Messrs Kynoch, who then despatched the ordered rounds to their London Warehouse, and from there, on to Major Spink.

Major Spink had a licence to shoot elephants which had expired on 28 February 1914. The licence enabled him to shoot two elephants a year, which was looked upon by the government officials as a sort of perquisite, allowing them to supplement their wages by an extra £200 to £300 by selling the ivory of the slain elephants.

Once back in Amadi he got together his expedition, which consisted of native bearers and equipment, and made his plans for going deeper into the country, to look for the two elephants he was going to shoot. He was in receipt of his recently ordered ammunition, which were all labelled as tropical cartridges. He tried one packet of them, all of the rounds appearing to be of a sufficient standard. He took a further four packets and moved further up country. On 15 February 1914, he shot a bull elephant, but only wounded the animal. He fired further shots, but although striking the beast, none of the rounds had penetrated the animal's thick skin. On closer inspection he noticed that instead of the bullets being solid they were in effect soft nose bullets, which deflected off the animal like stones thrown against a brick wall. He estimated that by having to abandon the expedition, he had lost between £130 and £140, but thankfully this also meant that no elephants were killed.

A real danger for those who took pleasure from killing elephants for their ivory, or sport, was that an elephant was a very powerful, as well as a very dangerous, beast. An elephant could detect the scent of a human 1,000 yards away, some distance before the human could spot or shoot at it. This gave the elephant the advantage, providing it remained quiet. The reason the matter was before the County Court in Birmingham, was not to charge with Major Spink with any offence, but for him to sue Messrs Kynoch, the company who supplied him with the ammunition. Judgment was reserved.

It seems somewhat short-sighted, through today's eyes, to carry on killing elephants, when the need for their raw strength and power would be a much-needed commodity that very same year. But it was a different world, and a time when ivory was much-desired by those in society who could afford it.

September 1915 also showed that the cost of looking after elephants, for whatever purpose, was most definitely not cheap by anyone's standards.

Two elephants, although helpful in the war effort, came at a cost. To wash and brush them down cost their owners more than £100, a huge sum of money back in 1915, hence why the occasion only took place once a year. Over 300lb of special soap had to be used in the process to thoroughly scrub their tough skin. Next they had to be walked into a nearby lake so that the soap could then be completely washed off. But that wasn't the end of the matter, far from it. Eight men then had to spend a week carefully rubbing gallons of special oil into the elephants' tough hides, which came at a hefty price.

One of the most important parts of the overall procedure was the cleaning out of the elephants' large, flat ears. This was done with the use of a hard, long-fibred brush. Their giant toes were also given careful treatment, which included the filing of their nails. If they were expected to carry out arduous work over long periods of time, their owners needed to ensure that they were in peak health and fitness, and free of any illness or diseases.

October 1915 brought with it an interesting story about elephants and their effect on the war.

An officer of the Flying Column of the West Riding Regiment, which had just finished a month's tour of the regimental districts, tells a story of how he secured a recruit for the Field Artillery, at the expense of his own unit. The officer saw a likely looking lad whilst he was recruiting in the market place at Otley. He engaged the young man in conversation and reminded him that he had a duty to his king and country to enlist and join the fight, if he was in fact fit and healthy enough to do so. The young man seemed suitably impressed but was also very cautious and did not immediately respond, whilst staring intently at the officer's cap and uniform. The officer could not understand the young man's prolonged silence, and asked him why he lingered in his reply.

West Riding Officers' Badges.

The young man eventually responded; 'Well, I'd like to join the army, but I don't want to go in your lot.'

'What's the objection?' asked the somewhat surprised officer, before at once proudly relating the glorious traditions of his own regiment.

'It's like this,' explained the young man. 'I've been used to horses all my life, but I don't know about elephants.'

Officers of the West Riding Regiment wore regimental badges on their shoulders which depicted elephants. An obvious mistake for the young man to have made. The recruiting officer got his man, but signed him up as a driver in the Royal Field Artillery.

The connection with elephants possibly comes from the Duke of Wellington's Regiment, which was formed from an amalgamation of the 33rd and 76th Regiment of Foot. The latter had been raised by the Honourable East India Company for service in India.

Elephants were most definitely used to assist the war effort during the First World War by both the Allies and Germany. In the main this came about as a result of necessity. Horses, or what horses were left, were few and far between. What made elephants appealing was that one of them could possibly undertake the work of what would have normally required four to six horses to complete.

To cover the gap and the work load left by horses, elephants were commandeered from zoos and circuses to carry out much needed war work. It was relatively straightforward for just one elephant to be able to cope with hauling loads of 8 tons and above, such was their brute strength. They were used in Sheffield to haul heavy loads. At a farm in Surrey, one was used to help plough the fields at planting time.

In January 1916, a Sheffield firm took on a new recruit, which came in the form of a huge elephant by the name of Lizzie. She was used for the hauling of the company's heavily laden lorries, a sight which interested many local people and one which raised curiosity for the reason behind the idea of having an elephant doing such work. Some were quite concerned how Lizzie's presence would affect the future of motor vehicles and the importance of the horse in a post-war Great Britain.

The elephant was a fine animal, girded in her massive harness, and attached by means of a pair of giant shafts to a large wooden waggon that was specifically designed for hauling heavy industrial loads, and bearing the name of Messrs T.W. Ward Ltd. She plodded along at what could only be described as a pedestrian pace, but with deliberation and a somewhat look of seriousness emblazoned across her face. The work was literally a stroll in the park, or to be more precise, a walk along the road. She did with consummate ease what five willing horses would have found tiresome at best.

The elephant was owned by Mr Sedgwick, the owner of a travelling menagerie, which was not a rarity for the time, as they would be today. The connection with Sheffield came about for no other reason than that is where the menagerie just happened to be at the time of the need of the elephant's very individual and unique skills. Mr Sedgwick became aware of a particular haulage need that Messrs Ward had, so a meeting was arranged, a display of what the elephant was capable of was given, and an agreement was made. The rest, as they say, is history. Lizzie was taken on the staff payroll on a temporary basis, and Messrs Ward were suitably impressed with her work.

She was 28 years of age, and although no spring chicken, still youthful enough to be easily able to do the work that was asked of her, as she happily plodded along the slightly hilly roads of Sheffield. It was a deceptive beast at first glance, because despite its movement appearing to be somewhat ponderous and slow, it still managed a speed of around 6 miles per hour, which was not to be scoffed at, especially when taking into account the weight of the loads that were being hauled.

The elephant idea was more a case of 'needs must' at the time, but it worked, and it was a pleasant alternative for Lizzie, even if it was only temporary.

In April 1916, another report appeared in the newspapers of a similar endeavour. This time the company concerned was Thomas Oxley Ltd, of the Shildon Works, Stanley Street, Sheffield. The report included a photograph of three heavy industrial boilers being hauled, as part of a government contract, on the back of a large wooden carriage with the company name emblazoned along each side. Hauling the heavy load was an elephant, although we have no way of knowing if it was Lizzie, and two camels. The article did not include the particulars of where they originated from.

May 1916 saw an extremely unusual jumble sale take place at the Caledonian market war fair in Pentonville, London. The jumble sale was organised by Lady Muriel Evelyn Vernon Paget, a philanthropist and humanitarian relief worker, in an effort to raise funds for the Wounded Allies' Relief Committee. Such was Lady Paget's social network that the Queen Mother, the Princess Royal, and other female members of the Royal Family attended the occasion to offer their support. These included the Duchess of Rutland and her daughter Lady Diana, along with Miss Elizabeth Asquith. As could be seen by the names of some of those who were openly supporting the event, this was not going to be just any ordinary jumble sale. As if to prove this point, two of the items that were on sale were an elephant and a giraffe.

The idea of unusual animals had obviously taken off in Sheffield in a big way. In June 1916, and possibly influenced by other elephant-related stories from the steel city, Mr John Hopwood, who managed a large dairy farm at Sandygate in Sheffield, as well as farming nearly 400 acres at Langold Netwell, Worksop, 20 miles away, was on the lookout for an elephant to undertake heavy harness work. Heavy vehicular traffic was almost constant on the roads between his two farms, and because of war-time restrictions, it was almost impossible to obtain one horse let alone any more than that, and a tractor was even harder to acquire.

Mr Hopwood believed that an elephant would be a natural for ploughing the fields, being capable of creating numerous furrows in one sweep, rather than the single one capable by a horse doing the same work. Mr Hopwood saw the possibility of harnessing a working elephant to not one, but three ploughs. Besides being useful on the land, it could also be utilised just as effectively pulling heavy loads on the roads.

This was in fact Lizzie, the same elephant who had worked for Messrs Ward and at the time of the sale was working for, and was still under contract to, Thomas Oxley Ltd. Once she had finished her commitments to Thomas Oxley, Mr Hopwood was very keen to give her a trial on his land, one that he believed would be very successful.

Friday, 7 December 1917, saw Alfredo Rossi, the owner of Rossi's Musical Elephants, appear at a West London Court to answer a charge that he had ill-treated a performing elephant. The case had been brought by the Royal Society for the Prevention of Cruelty to Animals, and related to an allegation that he had ill-treated one of his performing elephants, named Daisy, on 7 November 1917, at the Shepherd's Bush Empire.

It was alleged that Daisy had twice fallen on her way to the theatre, and was unable to carry out her expected tricks, which was quite possibly down to the fact that before the start of the journey, the animal had been given three bottles of whiskey. Having finally arrived to carry out her performance it was claimed that one of her attendants goaded her with a short spike, although Mr Boyd, the magistrate, said that having heard all of the evidence, he was happy that the attendant did not prod the animal with anything other than a wooden stick. Between the time of the performance and the matter coming to court, Daisy had unfortunately died, how that had come about wasn't something that was agreed upon between the defence and the prosecution.

Mr T.W. Chamberlain, a veterinary surgeon, told the court that an examination of Daisy's body showed that she had died of pneumonia. Mr F.H. Stainton, a veterinary surgeon for the defence, also made a post-mortem examination of Daisy, but he claimed that in his opinion, the elephant had not died of pneumonia, but of heart disease, and that the congestion of the lungs was a secondary factor.

The remaining three elephants owned by Mr Rossi were brought to court and inspected by Mr Boyd, which caused great interest and no amount of attention outside of the courts where crowds had gathered to see such an unusual spectacle.

Professor Woodridge, a consulting veterinary surgeon from the Zoological Society, stated that elephants could be very temperamental beasts and it was usual for them to show their annoyance by lying down. He had only known of one occasion when an elephant had fallen or laid down through illness, to have got up again.

In finding the case proven by the Royal Society for the Prevention of Cruelty to Animals, Mr Boyd said he found it hard to believe that Rossi would not have known that one of his elephants had serious health problems. He was found guilty of animal cruelty and fined the sum of £5, with a further 5 guineas to pay in court costs.

It seemed somewhat at odds with the time that four elephants, who could have been far better employed engaged in the nation's war effort on the home front, either whilst in private ownership or by being commandeered by the government, were being used in a show where their main purpose was to make lots of money for their owners whilst, if the evidence is to be believed, being cruelly treated by some of those entrusted with their wellbeing.

Chapter 3

Cavalry and Other Horses

The skill with this chapter is to make sure that the main focus stays on the horses themselves and not the men who rode them. Having said that, there will undoubtedly be times where the two cross over, because they are intrinsically linked with one another, but where they do, we will keep sight of the fact that it is the story of the horse that holds prominence.

At the time of the First World War, there were 32 cavalry regiments in the British Army, which each comprised 26 officers and 523 men of the other ranks, and each man requiring a horse. That comes to a

British Cavalry Officer leading his troop.

total of 17,568 horses. By the time of the Second World War, there were only 5 cavalry regiments left, the rest having been converted into either mechanised or armoured units.

Here is one of those times mentioned in the first paragraph where men and horses will be discussed on equal terms. Cavalry horses and their riders were involved in two really significant incidents in the First World War.

To set the scene, it was 22 August 1914, and 'C' Squadron of the 4th (Royal Irish) Dragoon Guards had been tasked with protecting the road that connected Mons with the neighbouring town of Soignies, near to the village of Casteau. 'C' Squadron had split, with two of the troops dismounting to take up ambush positions, whilst the remaining two troops had stayed mounted, but out of sight so as to be able to keep an element of surprise. At just after 6am, four German Lancers of the 4th Cuirassiers, who were part of the German 9th Cavalry Division, and part of an advanced guard of General Alexander von Kluck's 1st Army, were in the process of advancing on Mons. As the Lancers made their way down the road and were approaching the village of Casteau, something spooked their horses, which in turn alerted their troopers, and they decided to retreat. No sooner had they done so when Captain Hornby and his two troops broke cover and gave chase. The German Lancers were soon back with the main body of their force, safely as they thought. Not at all perturbed by the larger enemy force he now found himself up against, Hornby and his men charged, with their swords drawn, closing in on the enemy with every stride their horses made. In no time at all they were in amongst the Lancers, with their swords swinging and slashing, as the shocked and somewhat surprised Germans slowly took stock of the situation they found themselves in.

At 6.20am on 22 August 1914, near the Belgian village of Casteau, Drummer Ernest Edward Thomas, known as Edward, and serving with the 4th (Royal Irish) Dragoon Guards, dismounted from his horse, and began firing, one of his rounds striking and wounding a German soldier. This action resulted in him being credited with having fired the first British shot of the war. Sadly, history has not recorded the name of the horse, or whether it survived the war. As for Drummer Thomas, who had first enlisted in the army in 1898 with the Royal Horse Artillery, he did. He continued his service after the war, all the way through until 1923, having been mentioned in despatches, and awarded the Military Medal.

Charles Beck Hornby
(Museum of the Royal
Dragoon Guards)

Captain Charles Beck Hornby DSO JP, also of the 4th (Royal Irish) Dragoon Guards, has been credited with being the first British soldier to kill a German soldier during the war. This took place on the same day, and as part of the same location as Drummer Thomas's action, and just ten minutes later at 6.30am. He killed the unsuspecting German with his sword. For his actions that day, Hornby was awarded the Distinguished Service Order, but just three weeks later he was badly wounded, though survived. By the time the war was over he had twice been Mentioned in Despatches, and was awarded the Croix de Guerre. He survived the war and eventually retired from the army in 1922 at the rank of major. During the Second World War he re-enlisted in the army and served as a captain with the 4th/7th Royal Dragoon Guards, which by then was part of the Armoured Corps. He served between February 1941 and April 1943.

The first significant action of the First World War therefore involved a number of cavalry horses of the British Army.

What has subsequently been recorded in history as one of the great cavalry charges of the First World War took place on 14 July 1916, in the cornfields of High Wood, and involved elements of the 20th Deccan Horse of the Indian cavalry and the 7th Dragoon Guards of the British Army, as they gallantly charged towards the German lines.

The wood was on a ridge, and whoever held that ground had a significant advantage over all the surrounding area. At its peak the ridge at High Wood was a good 100 feet higher than the area which it overlooked. On 14 July, just two weeks into the Battle of the Somme, elements of the 7th Dragoon Guards, and the 20th Deccan Horse of the 2nd Indian Cavalry Division were called forward at 7:40am, but as they had to traverse a combination of trenches and uneven ground to get there, it was not a straightforward exercise. This was the first cavalry charge by British, Commonwealth or Allied troops since trench warfare had begun.

It would be the men and horses of the 20th Deccan Horse who would subsequently make the charge on the ridge at High Wood at about 7pm, against German Infantry of the 3rd Battalion, 26th Regiment. The 20th Deccan Horse powered their way up the incline, which in itself must have been an impressive sight. The combination of a large group of massive charging horses, steam blowing from their nostrils as their riders screamed at the top of their voices, swords drawn and pointing towards them would have been a terrifying sight for the young German soldiers in their path. By the time the charge was over, some 100 defenders lay dead, with many more who had been wounded. As for the 20th Deccan Horse, just 8 of their number had been killed, but more than 100 of them had been wounded. The horses, sadly, didn't fare so well, with 130 of them either killed or wounded.

The Commonwealth War Graves Commission website only records four men of the 20th Deccan Horse who were killed on 14 July 1916, and even more surprisingly, none of them have a known place of burial, which suggests that their bodies were not recovered from the battlefield, although the reason why that would have been the case is unclear. However, they were all commemorated on the Neuve-Chapelle Memorial.

The following is a message that was recorded along with the War Diary of the 20th Deccan Horse, which covers the date of this encounter. Rather than trying to interpret anything contained within it, it has been recorded here directly as it is shown in the diary. Hopefully it all makes sense.

> Move at once with your right on line cross roads 250 x N. of V in LONGUEVAL & S II Central into a position to attack DELVILLE WOOD from the North & North West so as to enable the 9th Division to complete the capture of that place. Your left via the Quarry in S. 22. C & Windmill 300 x N. of the G in LONGUEVAL. On arrival on the Ridge in S II to push forward strong patrols towards FLERS.
>
> Be sure to maintain Communication with the 7th D. Gds on your left & also with 9th Division on your right.
>
> G.O.C will move slightly to the rear of & between you and 7th D. Gds.

This message was timed at 7:30pm on 14 July 1916, although the actually entry in the 20th Deccan Horse War Diary for 14 July 1916 reads as follows. It is quite meagre in its content, but is all that the entry for 14 July 1916, actually includes.

> 1.30am – Assembles and arrived at BRAY at about 3.45am. Left BRAY at about 8.30am and with one half arrived in valley half a mile south of MONTAUBAN.
>
> 5.45pm – Received orders to move to a position of assembly at SABOT COPSE report marked A. Forwarded to 4th Brigade 16.7.16."
>
> 11pm onwards – The Regiment started assisting in and preparing a line of defence from S 10 Central & S. East across valley to S10 CO2, order from left to right B.A.D.C. Enemy scout shot by C Sq on listening post.

Further to this is a list of the names of those killed and wounded in the charge. It shows that three men were killed in action. Five men subsequently died of their wounds over the following few days. Sadly, there was no mention anywhere that could be found of the number of horses that had been killed in the attack.

During the war, all but one of the thirty-two regular army cavalry regiments saw action either in battles or fighting on the Western Front, or during the Mesopotamia campaign, although to many the cavalry were a thing of the past, from a bygone era, especially with the advancements and killing capabilities of the newly developed artillery pieces, which by the beginning of the First World War, were being produced on an industrial scale.

In essence, the war saw big changes, not just for the British, but for all combatant nations, in the use of their military tactics. What was clear to most, was that the time of the cavalry being the main stay of military tactics was fast coming to an end. At the beginning of the war, they still had their place in the greater scheme of things, but by the end of the war their effectiveness as a fighting force had greatly diminished.

They had become marginalised, and the more the war continued, the more they were used in support of main infantry units. Although still on horseback, they would often be dismounted and used as additional infantrymen; mainly as machine gunners or as small artillery units. There was still a driving force to use cavalry as cavalry, but this wasn't necessarily out of any tactical need, it was more to do with the fact that many of the officers who held senior command positions in the British Army had started out their military careers as cavalrymen, and subsequently remained loyal to the cause.

During the course of the First World War, there were only two commander-in-chiefs of the British Expeditionary Force. Between 1914 and 1915, the position was held by General John French, and between 1915 and 1918 the responsibility was taken over by Field Marshal Douglas Haig. Both men had begun their military careers as cavalry officers.

Field Marshal Edmund Henry Hynman Allenby, 1st Viscount Allenby, who was the first commander of the British Cavalry Division, went on to become the commander-in-chief of the Egyptian Expeditionary Force between 1917 and 1919. The five commanders of the British Armies on the Western Front were cavalry men. There were ten different corps that were commanded by cavalry men, and a further twenty-seven served as divisional commanders.

The cavalry influence in the British Army was very much alive and kicking throughout the years of the First World War, especially the initial ones.

A number of decorations for bravery were awarded to cavalry men throughout the war; these included eight who were awarded the

Victoria Cross. Three of these awards came about due to acts of bravery in the very first month of the war. By the end of the fighting 5,600 cavalrymen had been killed.

Cavalry charge of Burkel

As the title of this book suggests, it is about animals, and not one particular nation. To that end it is only right to mention the use of animals by other nations who were involved in the war, regardless of which side they were fighting on.

During the hundred days' offensive, which took place across the Western Front between 8 August and 11 November 1918, there was what has been recognised as the last cavalry charge of the First World War. It is referred to as the cavalry charge of Burkel, although it actually took place between the Belgium town of Oedelem and the nearby municipality of Maldegem. It was a skirmish between Belgian and German troops, which took place on 19 October 1918.

By this stage of the war, the Belgian Cavalry Division was stationed on the Western Front, but used in an infantry capacity, whilst their horses were kept back from the immediate front line and used for supply purposes.

In October 1918, with just over three weeks before the fighting finally came to an end with the signing of the Armistice, Belgian forces were advancing into positions which had been lost to the German Army in late 1914. Still, at this late stage of proceedings, Germany, although by now retreating at rapid speed towards her homeland, wasn't giving up without a fight.

The Belgian Army was fast becoming an unstoppable force, as Germany trundled closer and closer to defeat. The 5th Belgian Infantry Division finally reached Bruges on 18 October, whilst the 7th Belgian Infantry Division had managed to capture the town of Oostkamp the same day. In the meantime, the Belgian Cavalry Division had been ordered to attack the Belgian town of Ecklo, but had been prevented from doing so by the retreating Germans blowing up bridges at Ruddervoorde. Instead they were held in support behind the 1st Belgian Infantry Division, which was situated slightly to the west of Ruddervoorde.

The Germans, obviously having realised their position was becoming more and more tenuous, used the cover of darkness during the course of the night of 18/19 October 1918 to make good their escape, but the Belgian Army was determined not to let them escape. The Belgian Cavalry Division were ordered by their senior officers to mount up and give chase. One of the columns was held up on the outskirts of Burkel, when they came under attack from elements of the German rear guard, who were covering their colleagues' retreat. The Belgians had no option but to dismount, and fight as infantry.

On the afternoon of 19 October 1918, two squadrons of the 1st Regiment of Guides, an armoured regiment of the Belgian Army, were ordered to manoeuvre themselves into position to attack the Germans at Burkel from the rear, but for this to be achieved, they had to cut through the German lines by surprise, which was a tall order for anybody. The Guides encountered withering machine-gun fire from the German defenders. With the element of surprise lost, Belgian forces used their artillery to create a breach in the German defensive lines.

There then followed what must have been one of the most confusing sights for a defending force to have ever been confronted with. Through the clearing caused by the Belgian artillery in the forest of Burkel came two armoured vehicles of the 1st Regiment of Guides, followed closely behind by Lancers of the Belgian Cavalry Division. The plan worked and the first line of German trenches was quickly taken, although this did end the usefulness of the Belgian armoured vehicles, which having arrived at the trench system, could go no further.

The second line of German trenches was nearly 2 miles further on, and although the Belgian Cavalry speedily made their way to their next objective, the element of surprise had been well and truly lost, and the German machine-gunners lay in wait for them.

Thankfully the Belgian Cavalry did not continue their charge, and by doing so rode blindly to their deaths. Instead they were ordered to dismount, leaving their horses out of harm's way. They continued on foot, fighting as infantry. So effective were they that by late afternoon the Germans gave up their positions and continued their retreat.

To end the piece on cavalry, here is a fitting a poem from an unnamed member of the Royal Scots Greys Cavalry Regiment.

A Cavalry Charger

I'm only a cavalry charger,
And I'm dying as fast as I can,
For my body is riddled with bullets,
They've potted both me and my man.
And though I've no words to express it,
I'm trying this message to tell
To kind folks who work for the Red Cross,
Oh please help the Blue Cross as well.

My master was one in a thousand,
And I loved him with all this poor heart,
For horses are built just like humans,
Be kind to them, they'll do their part.
So please send out help for our wounded,
And give us a word in your prayers;
This isn't so strange as you'd fancy,
The Russians do it in theirs.

I'm only a cavalry charger,
And my eyes are becoming quite dim,
I really don't mind, though I'm done for,
So as long as I'm going to him;
But first I would plead for my comrades,
Who're dying and suffering, too,
Oh, please help the poor wounded horses!
I'm sure that you would if you knew.

Horses in general

The First World War began just twelve years after the end of the Second
Boer War, or the South African War, as it was also referred to, which raged
between 1899 and 1902. This was a war that had been heavily reliant on the
use of horses, and in the three years of fighting, the British Army had used
520,000 of them. Out of these, more than 320,000 of them died, just over
60 per cent. What is even sadder is that the majority of those deaths were

not as a result of enemy action, but as a result of exhaustion or disease. This suggests that many of the horses who died did so unnecessarily as their deaths would have been preventable. What makes these losses even more incredible and harder to understand, is that the Army Veterinary Department was in existence at that time, having been formed in 1880. Lessons had been learned though, and in 1903, just one year after the end of the Second Boer War, the Army Veterinary Corps was formed, which was somewhat greatly enlarged from its predecessor, the Army Veterinary Department.

At the beginning of the First World War, the British Army was short of everything; men, vehicles and animals. The history of the automobile could be traced back to 1769 when the French inventor, Nicholas-Joseph Cugnot, built the world's first steam-powered land-based automobile that people could ride upon. It was 1885 before German engine designer and automobile engineer, Karl Friedrich Benz, produced an automobile which ran on petrol and was powered by a single cylinder four stroke engine. But it wasn't until 1913, just one year before the start of the war, that the Ford Model T became the first mass-produced automobile. It will therefore come as no surprise to hear that the British Army was still heavily reliant on good old-fashioned horse power to be able to fight its war. They were used to transport heavy artillery, men, equipment, ammunitions, fuel, post, food, wounded soldiers, and basically anything else that might be needed to fight the war.

Army Remount Service

At the beginning of the war the British Army had the comparatively small number of 25,000 horses and mules, which was obviously never going to be sufficient to sustain the entire war. The Army Remount Service got straight to work and in less than two weeks after the war had begun, they had secured a further 140,000 horses and mules. By August 1915, that number had increased to 534,971, and by 1917 the British Army had acquired a total of 870,000, which is an absolutely staggering number.

The Army Remount Service had the power to impress horses for public service. It was their job not only to purchase horses and mules, but to train them as well. They had first come in to being in 1887, and prior to this time the task of purchasing such animals lay with the colonel of individual regiments. In 1891, it became part of the Army Service Corps.

The idea behind the Remount section was uniformity in the horses that were purchased for the army and to ensure the training they were subsequently given. Farmers and individuals who owned horses were encouraged, as it was not compulsory, to register a number of their horses with the Army Remount Service, which would then give the army the option of purchasing those animals for an agreed amount of money, should the situation require it.

At the outbreak of the First World War the Army Remount Service had seven depots. There were two in Dublin for the cavalry and one at Woolwich in London, which was responsible for the purchase of horses for the Royal Artillery, the Royal Engineers, and the Army Service Corps. A fourth was situated at Melton Mowbray, in Leicestershire, and a fifth was at Aborfield Garrison in Berkshire. There was also a sixth at Pickard's Farm in the village of Chiddington, near Godalming in Surrey, the owners of which had given the land to the War Office with a lease of twenty-one years. As the war continued and even more horses were required for military purposes, four more depots were opened to help cope with this extra demand. These were at Shirehampton, near Bristol, Romsey, a market town in Hampshire, Ormskirk, which is also a market town, in West Lancashire, and Swathling, in Southampton on the south coast. In addition to these, other Remount Depots were set up in France, as well as Egypt and Salonika.

The Army Remount Service was only responsible for the purchase and training of horses within Britain. Those needed by the Indian Army were sourced and paid for by the Indian Government. The purchase of horses used in other theatres of war was the responsibility of each of the local general officers in command.

The government and the War Office certainly appeared to be taking animal welfare seriously. An example of this was the number of men it had allocated to the Army Remount Service. At the outbreak of the war, the unit was staffed by 121 officers and 230 men. War Office figures show that in 1917, these numbers had risen to 423 officers and 20,560 men. Most of the officers of the Army Remount Service were drawn from the landed gentry and masters of fox hounds, and others who had experience of working with horses in civilian life, in an effort to try and reduce the numbers of officers taken from the regular British Army.

The Army Remount Service did a remarkable job under demanding and difficult conditions. By the end of the war they had purchased a total of 468,323 horses throughout the United Kingdom, a further 428,608 horses and 275,097 mules from North America, 6,000 horses and 1,500 mules came from South America, along with 3,700 mules that were purchased from Spain and Portugal. The cost of purchasing and training all of these animals, in the six years between 1914 and 1920 came to £67.5 million, which at today's value, comes to roughly £4.5 billion.

Besides the British Army, the Remount Service also purchased horses and mules for Australia, Belgian, Canada, Portugal and New Zealand.

By the end of the war, British forces alone had lost 480,000 horses, which was roughly one horse to every two British soldiers who were killed or died.

Royal Army Veterinary Corps

In 1903, an Army Veterinary Corps was founded, which employed men specifically to look after army horses. In 1906, it merged with the already established Army Veterinary Department, and collectively they became the Royal Army Veterinary Corps.

This all came about in the aftermath of the Second Boer War, 1899–1902, after the British public were outraged over the deaths of hundreds of thousands of army horses.

As an operational unit of the British Army, it is still responsible for the provision, training and care of its animals. During the course of the

Royal Army
Veterinary Corps
Cap Badge.

First World War, it did not have the prefix of 'Royal'. This was only used from 27 November 1918, and was awarded to commemorate the excellent work carried out by the corps during the war.

When the First World War began, the corps had 364 officers combined in both the Regular and Reserve armies, along with 934 men. These figures increased throughout the war, and by the time the fighting had finished, there had been a total of 1,670 officers and 41,755 men who had served with the corps. This either displays the level of care afforded to the animals, or the greater number of personnel that it took to look after such an ever-increasing number of sick and wounded animals. Either way, it showed a caring and well-deserved commitment to a body of animals, without whose help winning the war would have been a lot harder to achieve.

There were 71 Mobile Veterinary Sections during the First World War, each of which could cater for up to 2,000 animals at any given time. In essence this meant that for every division that left the United Kingdom to go and serve overseas, each had a veterinary unit that went with it. In addition to these, there were also a number of base veterinary hospitals, two of which were at Le Havre and Rouen.

A Mobile Veterinary Section, in simple terms, was a first aid station for animals, although the reality of this was that in nearly every case they were dealing with horses. Each of these sections provided medical care for the division it was attached to; for sick, wounded or injured horses. Typically the ailments they were treated for were bullet or shrapnel wounds, exhaustion, mange, and exposure to gas attacks, many of which were chlorine-related. Those that required greater care were sent to the nearest Base Veterinary Hospital.

Each of the Mobile Veterinary Sections was staffed by a minimum of twenty-four men. This included one veterinary officer, two sergeants, one corporal, one shoeing smith, two batmen, one driver – who in nearly all cases was supplied by the Army Service Corps – and sixteen privates. They were also allocated sixteen horses. One for a cart, two draught, and the remainder for general riding.

If ever a unit of the British Army proved its worth, it was the men of the Royal Army Veterinary Corps. During the course of the war they treated an estimated 2.5 million horses and mules. Of these, 2 million were fit enough to 'return to work' at what they had been doing before they were injured or became sick. Although that was a remarkable achievement, it also sadly meant that some half-a-million of them had to be 'put to sleep.' In each case it was done humanely, in line with the level of respect and love that was felt for them by those who treated and looked after them.

During the Battle of Verdun in 1916, which saw the French and German armies pitted against one another, an estimated 7,000 horses were killed as a result of artillery shelling.

Sadly, after the end of the First World War, the Royal Army Veterinary Corps began to wind down its overall operation, and the level of its personnel was also greatly reduced, in keeping, it could be argued, with the reduction in need for military horses because of the increased use of mechanised vehicles. This reduction in the ranks of the Royal Army Veterinary Corps continued throughout the 1930s, to such an extent that in 1938, the Royal Army Veterinary School, which was situated in Aldershot, closed its doors for the very last time.

With the rise of Nazism throughout Germany, a second world war was always just a matter of when, rather than if. With that in mind, and with the benefit of hindsight, the massive reduction of the Royal Army Veterinary Corps could be recorded historically as a bad decision. The effect of this was that at the start of the Second World War, the corps only had 26 officers in England, along with 105 men from the other ranks, although there were a further 59 officers stationed and working in India.

A couple of very interesting statistics concerning the Royal Army Veterinary Corps. A total of 207 men who served with the corps died during the First World War, but 206 of them died after the signing of the Armistice on 11 November 1918.

Forty-one died between 12 November and 31 December 1918. Between 1 January and 31 December 1919, 134 died, 24 died between 1 January and 31 December 1920, and 7 died between 1 January and 31 December 1921.

Another man, Private 75 Diri Hershi, is commemorated on the Screen Wall Memorial Garden 'B' at the Dar Es Salaam War Cemetery in Tanzania. The slightly odd thing about his death is that it is not known how, when or where the man died. His official date of death is recorded as sometime between 4 August 1914 and 31 August 1921, but no explanation could be found as to the circumstances surrounding his death.

As the war entered its final year, there was a very interesting discussion amongst MPs in the House of Commons as the Horse Breeding Bill was having its second reading. The date was 30 April 1918. The Bill was the work of Mr Prothero, President of the Board of Agriculture, that of the Secretary for Scotland, and the Secretary of Ireland. The purpose of the Bill was to regulate the use of stallions travelling for hire, or exhibited in certain places, markets or shows, and after the appointed day to prohibit any stallion without a licence from travelling, or from being exhibited.

During the war the British Army bought a number of light and heavy horses, and the subsequent reports that were written by the Remount officers did not exactly make for good reading, in fact they disclosed a very worrying state of affairs. A letter from the War Office was quoted in the report of the committee that had been appointed by the President of the Board of Agriculture to consider the supply of horses for military purposes. That report was published three years earlier in 1915. Page five of the report contained the following paragraph:

> The War Office wrote on the 13th December 1914 as follows: 'Owing, however, to the inferiority of many of the sires, a large number of these horses are of so poor a stamp as to be of no military value, and the Council regard it as of the utmost importance that steps should at once be taken to arrest the deterioration of the light draught horse stock in this country.

The same Committee received a letter on 9 July 1915, which included the following paragraph:

> Unhappily the experience of the recent mobilisation has proved that though this country produces many super excellent horses, the number of unsound and utterly worthless animals, which ought never to have been bred, is deplorably large.

A well-known expert of the day, who had been one of the most successful breeders of Shire horses for the previous thirty years, publicly expressed the opinion that at least 50 per cent of the horses employed upon farms were unsound. If that was the case it would have been of the utmost importance, both domestically and from a military point of view, to take steps to rectify and improve that situation expediently. The sooner the quality of the nation's horses could be improved, the better for all concerned. The starting point in this process was to eliminate those stallions that were determined as being unsound. A single stallion could sire fifty to sixty foals in a season and if they were unsound, the nation's breeding programme could have been inundated with unsound horses very quickly.

Looking back on this all these years later is quite chilling, as it seems that the War Office and senior officers in the British Army were well aware that a number of the horses they were purchasing were nowhere near up to the required standard. In doing so they were sending horses to the Western Front and further afield that should never have been sent there because they were not up to the job that they had been bought to do. In doing this, soldiers of the British Army were put at risk, and it most definitely wasn't fair for the horses either, some of whom weren't even deemed suitable to be undertaking work on a farm.

What is also of concern is that at the time of the First World War this was not a new problem. It had been first highlighted back in 1873, when a select committee expressed the opinion that a compulsory system needed to be put in place for the registration of all stallions throughout the country. Nothing came out of that recommendation, and twenty-three years later, there was the Advisory Committee on Horse Breeding. Still nothing was done.

In 1911, a grant was made by the Development Commission for the improvement of horse breeding, at which time a system of voluntary registration was put in place that allowed for stallions to be placed on the register after they had been thoroughly examined by a vet. This scheme attracted 1,900 voluntary registrations, but it still left hundreds more, who for whatever reason had not bothered to do so. It was definitely a step in the right direction

In 1915, there was the Lord Middleton Committee, which strongly recommended the compulsory registration of all stallions. The first of their conclusions was that the Board of Agricultural and Fisheries should institute any legislation required for the purpose of an annual registration of all stallions that travelled around the country at shows and displays. By 1918, this still had not been put in place.

It was more about who was a reputable breeder and who wasn't. For the reputable ones, being able to have a registered stallion cover one of their mares made perfect sense and meant that they would have little problem selling any subsequent foals, even though this meant having to pay more for the privilege. For the more unscrupulous, and dare I say, the more short-sighted breeders, having their mare covered as cheaply as possible was the more important factor just as long as they had a foal to subsequently sell, they didn't really care.

It was almost as if the First World War provided a kind of cleansing opportunity for the British horse breeding system. Wrap it all up in one big bundle, throw it away, and start all over again.

It is estimated that more than 6 million horses and mules, from all sides, were utilised during the course of the First World War, with almost 3 million of them dying. Of these, a larger percentage died as a result of diseases or ailments such as equine influenza, ringworm, sand colic, anthrax, cracked heels, frostbite, exhaustion and tsetse-related infection.

One of the other issues related to horses was feeding them. Horse fodder proved to be the largest single item shipped across the English Channel during the entire war. Feeding horses was more expensive than feeding soldiers, mainly because as a rule of thumb, horses would eat around ten times as much food by weight as a soldier would.

Whether Germany had realised that cutting off the supply of horse feed would reduce the effectiveness of British and Allied forces on the Western Front is an unknown factor, but intentionally or otherwise, that's what happened for a period of time after Germany re-introduced her policy of unrestricted submarine warfare in February 1917. This was when German submarines would attack, without warning, Allied freighters and tankers, especially those that were heading for British harbours. This tactic greatly restricted Allied supplies of oats and hay that was being shipped across from North America. This resulted in Britain having to ration the amount of feed that each of the horses was given. German horses also suffered food shortages, simply because whoever was responsible for the pre-war stockpiling of their animal feed for military purposes had miscalculated the amount needed.

Besides the use of horses for military purposes, they were also seen as a morale booster for the troops at the front. Being devoid of human love and affection was a major factor for a lot of the men, so having a horse that they could stroke, talk to or feed was a massive help. There was however a downside to this close contact and living side by side with each other. Put simply, wherever there were a number of horses there was lots and lots of manure. Although nominated sanitation officers were responsible for its burial, along with horse carcases, fast-moving battle conditions didn't always allow this to happen. Where there was manure, disease-carrying insects and flies were not that far away.

The end of the war brought with it what could be described as some of the worst treatment of horses throughout all the years of fighting. Instead of being shipped home to see out their years happily grazing in the fields, which they had in part kept out of the grasp of German hands, many of them were killed because of their age or illness. Those who were healthy and younger were sold to the French or the Belgians, or ended up in slaughterhouses.

Horses being fed.

Only 62,000 horses made it back to England after the war, and this only happened after the intervention of Winston Churchill, at a time when he was the minister for munitions in David Lloyd George's government.

Of the 136,000 horses shipped to Europe from Australia, only one made it back home. By the end of the war there were only 13,000 Australian horses who had survived. Of these, 2,000 were simply killed, whilst most of the remaining 11,000 ended up in India. The horses from New Zealand didn't fare any better. Those that were not required by the British or Egyptian armies, were simply shot. The reason given for this course of action was staggering. They were shot rather than sold, because the new owners might not treat them well. Unbelievable and extremely sad.

German horses didn't fare much better. They used 1.5 million horses throughout the war. Of these, an estimated 400,000 were killed as a result of direct enemy fire, or subsequently died of their wounds, but 0.5 million died of disease.

Chapter 4

Mascots

Mascots played a big part in the First World War, both official regimental animals and unofficial, yet widely-accepted ones, some of which were kept by individuals. In different ways, these animals were of great help to the men, which in some cases made for what some might describe as unusual combinations.

One of the strangest photographs on the subject, which can be seen overleaf, is that of a pilot from the 32nd Squadron Royal Air Force and a fox. The photograph was taken on 5 May 1918, at the Humieres Aerodrome, St Pol, France. The animal appears quite at ease and happy, and has clearly become a pet to either the pilot in the photograph or the pilot's squadron, and can be clearly seen wearing a collar and a lead, which is held by the pilot as the fox looks out from the rear of the aircraft's cockpit.

Raoul Lufbery was an American pilot serving in France during the First World War when he was photographed with a lion named Whiskey.

Forces Mascot. 15th Battalion, Welsh Regiment.

Above: Pilot with his Fox.

Right: Gervais Raoul Victor Lufbery.

The animal can quite clearly be seen wearing a collar as the two playfully engage with each other on the ground.

In the photograph below, a couple of soldiers, possibly serving with the Royal Field Artillery, or the Army Service Corps, slowly make their way to their destination with much-needed supplies and equipment. Not of course forgetting their tethered goat; it isn't made clear whether it is a pet, mascot, or dare I say, a meal at a later time. A goat could have quite easily been found by the troops as they made their way across the Western Front, who then decided to bring it with them, rather than leave it behind to an uncertain future. The two soldiers appear quite relaxed about the goat being behind them, although it does look like they have strategically placed a large sack full of supplies between themselves and the animal.

The South African Scottish Regiment had a pet baboon named Jackie as their unusual mascot, who they took to France with them when they sailed from South Africa. Jackie had both excellent eyesight and hearing and remained with the men when they were serving in the front line. This proved a useful addition as he was like an early-warning system, and would call out if he heard noise or movement coming from no man's land. It is claimed that he had excellent table manners, having copied what the men did when they were having their own meals

It could be said that one of the most famous mascots ever was Winnipeg, the black bear better known as Winnie. She had become an unofficial mascot to Canadian forces, who when it came to their turn to

Soldiers and their goat mascot.

be shipped out to France, left her at London Zoo until they returned. She quickly became a big attraction, especially as visitors could get close up and personal with her, which made her very endearing to the masses.

There is another interesting part of the story that needs telling, which is how Winnie came to be in England in the first place. Not surprisingly, the story begins in Canada; White River, Ontario to be precise.

At the outbreak of the First World War, Harry D. Colebourn was a lieutenant in the Fort Garry Horse, which was a Canadian cavalry regiment. He quickly volunteered for service and enlisted in the Canadian

Winnipeg the bear and Lieutenant Harry Colebourn.

Army Veterinary Corps. On his way to the Valcartier forces' base, which is about 15 miles north of Quebec City, the train he was on stopped at White River, Ontario. Whilst there, Colebourn possibly did the most unusual thing anybody who was en route to join up with his new military unit could have possibly done. He purchased a bear. Yes, you read that correctly, he purchased a small, black, female bear from a hunter for $20. As the young bear had constantly been with humans for nearly all of her young life, she was already domesticated in the art of human interaction.

Colebourn decided on the name Winnipeg, which in turn was quickly shortened to Winnie, after his home town of Winnipeg in Manitoba. I can only guess at how the conversation went when he arrived at the Valcartier Army base with a young, female bear in tow. Maybe because he was an officer the conversation was a totally different one to what it would have been if he had been a private soldier. Whoever the conversation was had with, it went well, because not only was he allowed to keep the bear,

Winnipeg and unknown soldier.

but it became the official mascot of the Canadian Army Veterinary Corps. When it was time for Colebourn to leave Canada, Winnie went with him in her official capacity as the corps mascot, and when they arrived in England, she became a pet to the staff of the Second Infantry Brigade headquarters.

When Colebourn had to leave England on his way to France as part of the Canadian Expeditionary Force, he knew that it simply was not practicable to take Winnie with him, so he arranged for her to stay at London Zoo, who were more than happy to look after her.

After the war, Colebourn fully intended to take Winnie back to Canada with him, where he meant for her to see out her days at the Assiniboine Park Zoo, in his home town of Winnipeg, but when Colebourn discovered how happy she was at London Zoo, and that she had become a much-loved attraction because of her playful and gentle manner, he changed his mind, and decided it was better for Winnie to remain where she was. She died at London Zoo on 12 May 1934, when she was 20 years of age.

So the story goes, that whilst Winnie was staying at London Zoo, the famous writer, Mr A.A. Milne, took his son, Christopher Robin, to see him. He was so taken by him that his father started writing stories about his son and Winnipeg, which subsequently became the now world famous *Winnie the Pooh* stories.

As for Harry Colebourn, it would be remiss to end this interesting story without providing a little bit more information about him. He was in fact English, having been born in Birmingham, England, on 12 April 1887, before emigrating to Canada with his family in 1905. He attended the Ontario Veterinary College, in the city of Guelph, where he earned a degree in veterinary surgery. With said qualification in hand, he moved to Winnipeg, looking for a job.

He survived the war, having reached the rank of major, but instead of returning to Canada he stayed in England and attended the Royal College of Veterinary Surgeons in London, where he carried out post-graduate work. He remained in England until 1920, before returning to Winnipeg, where he set up his own private practice. He died on 24 September 1947, aged 60, and is buried at the Brookside military cemetery, in Winnipeg.

Although many animals were abandoned to fend for themselves as French and Belgian families had to flee their homes to escape from the advancing German forces, it would appear from the collar around the animal's neck (see bottom image on page 46) that it had been taken on as a mascot, rather than something to eat.

The photograph on page 46, which was taken in France on 21 April 1918, shows a soldier from the New Zealand Engineers, with the regiment's mascot, an Egyptian goat named Nan. Where the connection between a New Zealand regiment and an Egyptian goat comes from, we cannot be sure.

Above left: Memorial of Winnipeg and Lieutenant Harry Colebourn at Assinboine Park Zoo, Winnipeg.

Above right: Headstone of Harry Colebourn.

45

A lance corporal of the Royal Scots Regiment with the regimental mascot.

A soldier of the New Zealand Engineers with the regimental mascot.

46

3rd Battalion (Toronto Regiment) Canadian Expeditionary Force – Mascot.

The 3rd Battalion (Toronto Regiment) Canadian Expeditionary Force was formed on 2 September 1914, and left for England just twenty-three days later on 25 September, on board the SS *Tunisia*. The journey took twenty-one days, before finally arriving in England on 16 October.

The 42 officers and the 1,123 men of the 3rd Battalion were glad to be back on dry land once again. They would later arrive in France and see action as part of the 1st Canadian Infantry Brigade, at Ypres and Vimy Ridge, as well as other locations along the Western Front. By the end of the war, besides those killed and wounded, the 3rd Battalion had a further 286 of its men captured and taken prisoner by the Germans.

The 3rd Battalion's official mascot from 1916 was a small black goat, who on ceremonial occasions was dressed in a miniature coat, which had the regiment's coat of arms emblazoned across both sides.

The 15th (Carmarthenshire) Battalion, Welsh Regiment, was formed in October 1914, and after having completed six months of basic training, it became part of the 129th Infantry Brigade, at Rhyl in North Wales.

Di the goat, 15th Battalion, Welsh Regiment Mascot.

The battalion undertook more training in Winchester, beginning in August 1915, before arriving in France in December 1915. Its mascot was a long-haired white goat named Di.

The 17th Battalion, Welsh Regiment, also known as the 1st Glamorgan Bantams, had a white goat as its mascot, but it was much smaller in size, and its name was Billy. As can be seen from the photograph opposite, the regimental coat the goat is wearing includes a bantam, and the spelling of the regiment's name is 'Welch'.

Those in the photograph from left to right are: Lieutenant Noel Evans, Mrs Dora Wilkie, Billy, and Colonel Charles Joseph Wilkie. The colonel was killed in action on 19 October 1916, and is buried at the Maroc British Cemetery at Grenay, in the Pas de Calais region of France.

Not surprisingly, Australian units during the First World War had kangaroos as their regimental mascots. Most regiments or corps left their mascots back home, or for those nations serving on the Western Front, in England, before crossing the English Channel. But as can be seen from the opposite photograph, under the shadow of the Egyptian pyramids, some Australian units, such as the 9th and 10th Battalions, Australian Infantry, at the Mena camp in Egypt, in December 1914, liked to take their mascots with them. Fortunately for the kangaroo, there wouldn't have been too much difference between the heat of an Egyptian desert and the dry and arid conditions it was used to back home.

Mascot of 17th Battalion, Welsh Regiment (From left to right) Lieutenant Noel Evans, Mrs Wilkie, Colonel C.J. Wilkie.

Kangaroo mascot with Australian soldiers in Egypt.

Kangaroo mascot in Egypt.

The kangaroo was not only a mascot for the Australians, it also played a big part in the nation's recruitment efforts, appearing on posters and postcards, as the authorities played on people's patriotism.

In an effort to help Australian soldiers recover from their wounds, there was even a kangaroo for a time at the No.1 Australian Auxiliary Hospital at Harefield Park House in Harefield, Middlesex. The property was actually owned by Australians, Mr and Mrs Charles Billyard-Leake, but they gave it up to be used for convalescent wounded soldiers of the AIF for the duration of the war. At the peak of its use, the hospital catered for more than one thousand patients, either officers or men.

It was common practice for regiments, corps, battalions and squadrons to have mascots during the First World War, as it had been for many years prior to the conflict, and in many cases there was no obvious or particular connection between the animal and the unit they were the mascot for. The Canadian Highland Regiment had a British Bulldog as its mascot. The London Scottish Regiment had a deerhound, the Royal Welsh Fusiliers had a long-haired white goat, presented to them by the Queen. The Princess Pats, a Canadian Regiment, had a brown bear as its mascot, whilst the Warwickshire Regiment had the slightly unusual Blackbuck and the Australian Victoria Rifles, a mounted unit, had a wallaby as a mascot.

Tame monkey dressed as a soldier.

In March 1915, the 2nd Battalion, 24th London Regiment, was presented with a white goat by the name of Peggy, by a Belgian lady at the Reigate and Redhill Horse and Hound Show, which was quickly taken to the hearts of the young men of the battalion.

In September 1915, the London Zoo was asked by a local magistrate to take in a bear. The zoo reluctantly declined the request on the grounds that it already had more bears than it could sensibly cater for. This was due to an influx of the animals that had arrived in the country with Canadian forces, who had brought them over as their official regimental mascots.

A bulldog named Caesar was the mascot of 'A' Company, 4th Battalion, New Zealand Rifle Brigade. He was also a Red Cross trained dog, who had been taught to help locate and rescue wounded troops on the battlefield. He was with his battalion as they took part in the Battle of the Somme, which began on 1 July 1916, where he was sadly killed. His collar can be found at the Auckland War Memorial Museum.

In recent times a book about his life, *Caesar the ANZAC Dog*, was written by Patricia Stroud and illustrated by Bruce Potter.

The New Zealand Army rugby team had a mascot, a bitch Fox Terrier named Floss, and she travelled with them when they played games in

Peggy the Goat.

several English cities during 1917. Floss was actually English and was given to one of the players, Driver Percy E. Lowndes, who proceeded to teach her a number of tricks.

When the team returned to New Zealand, Floss went with them, but when they eventually arrived in Wellington, the quarantine officers wouldn't let her into the country, but the New Zealand rugby team weren't defeated that easily, so they smuggled her in.

The New Zealand government paid to have a battle cruiser made for the British Royal Navy and she made her maiden voyage in 1913 and was aptly named HMS *New Zealand*. The ship's mascot was a bulldog puppy with the impressive name of Pelorus Jack, named after a dolphin that had swum alongside ships in the outer Marlborough Sounds at the northern end of the New Zealand's South Island. The dog sadly died in an unexplained incident on 24 April 1916, when he somehow managed to fall down one of the ship's funnels. The mystery was how he managed to get up so high in the first place.

Not only was the mascot replaced with a dog of the same breed, but it was given the exact same name as well. He survived the war, even the trauma of being on board the vessel when she took part in the Battle of Jutland.

The 5th (Reserve) Battalion, New Zealand Rifle Brigade arrived at Cannock Chase, near Brockton, in September 1917. Their mascot, Freda, a Great Dane, was by all accounts a friendly old girl, but how and when she actually became their mascot is open to some conjecture.

In the month between October and November 1918, and according to the Commonwealth War Graves Commission, fifty-seven members of the New Zealand Rifle Brigade died whilst serving in England. Most of the deaths were sadly down to the effects of the influenza pandemic that was sweeping across the world at the time. Sadly, another of victim of the flu was dear old Freda.

In essence, most battalions, regiments or corps had a mascot of some description or another during the First World War.

Chapter 5

Pets

There are three main aspects to be discussed on the topic of pets. Firstly, those people who gave up their pets so that they could be trained for military purposes, soldiers in the trenches or otherwise serving on the front line, and prisoners of war who kept pets.

Internee with
a baby crow

Alexandra Palace was not actually a prisoner of war camp, it was a civilian internment camp for men who were born in Austria, Germany and Hungary, and who prior to the war had lived and worked in the United Kingdom. Many of these men had married British women and raised families with them, but by 1914, and with the passing of the Aliens Restriction Act 1914, it was felt that these very same people could be a threat to Britain's national security, so they were locked up. When war initially broke out, it was determined that such individuals had to register with the police in the area in which they lived.

But it was not long before the British Government amended the Act and decided that all Austrian, German and Hungarian men aged between 17 and 55 years of age should be interned. A more salubrious location for these men to have been locked up in would have been hard to find.

At Alexandra Palace there was a poultry farm where – surprise, surprise – chickens were kept. They would have served four purposes. Some would have been kept as pets, some of the hens would have been used for breeding, whilst others would have provided a constant source of eggs which would have been consumed by the internees, and one could

Poultry Farm at Alexandra Palace.

Prisoner with his pet cat.

assume that some would have, no doubt, ended up providing much needed protein at meal times, though there is no actual evidence to support this.

In the photograph on the previous page, notice the armed guard standing to the right of two of the internees. That in itself was somewhat of a strange aspect to camp life. Armed guards covering the main entrance to the camp could be understood, as could armed guards in watchtowers. Armed guards patrolling outside of the perimeter fence could also be understood, but inside the camp does seem somewhat unusual.

In the photograph on page 54, the man in the pith hat appears to be holding a baby crow, which seems more than happy to be sitting in the palm of his hand. Although at first glance it might appear to be a strange combination, and certainly an unusual pet to keep, it goes to show that in difficult times, when men are separated from their families, their normal day-to-day routine, and are devoid of love and affection, the companionship of a pet of whatever shape or form can play a very big part in keeping them sane by filling the void and feelings of loneliness that men feel when separated from their families.

Prisoners of war were always going to face restrictions on the type of animals they would be allowed to keep as pets within their camps.

German POW
with his pet
rabbit.

Dogs certainly were never going to be anywhere near the top of the list
for permitted animals. The German prisoner of war in this photograph,
which was taken at the German PoW camp at Dorchester, appears to
be a very happy man as he poses with a rabbit, not a parrot, on his
shoulder. Such pets would have certainly needed looking after by those
who had decided to nurture them. Hunger and jealousy can do strange
things to a man's mind, particularly in such circumstances. I can see
how it could very quickly become a case of 'one man's pet is another
man's meal'.

The camp at Poundbury received its first prisoners on 10 August
1914, just a week after the war had started, and had in a previous life
been an artillery barracks for the British Army. It quickly filled up, and
to accommodate the PoWs a number of wooden huts, large enough to
cater for thirty men, were erected in the grounds of the camp. At its peak
the camp was home to some 4,500 men. How many of them kept pets is
not recorded.

Soldiers with rabbit and chicken. Maybe both pets and food.

One photograph, two soldiers, but a contrasting story. The man holding the chicken looks a lot happier about being photographed than his slightly larger, grimacing colleague with the rabbit. The small pot, which has been leaned up against the makeshift chicken coop, appears to have a number of eggs in it. The fate of the rabbit could be open for discussion for two reasons. Firstly, the larger pot appears to be full of boiling water, and the soldier holding the rabbit looks a lot better fed than his sergeant holding the chicken. Having said that, the sergeant could also be smiling because he knows what he will be having for his tea that evening.

Regardless of which pets were kept by soldiers at the front, it must have been a very difficult job to keep them alive. Many of the trenches, whether German or Allied, were infested with rats attracted by either sewage waste or dead bodies. Some of these rats were reportedly quite large, having feasted on the rotten corpses of soldiers lost in water-ridden shell holes in no man's land. What chance, therefore, did a defenceless chicken or rabbit have? Cats were also quite common in the trenches, mainly to keep on top of the plague of mice and rats that had made the front line their home. A chicken would have been no match for a determined cat.

Some men had their nerves shattered as a result of the constant hours of artillery bombardments that rained down on their defensive positions. These attacks also claimed the lives of many young soldiers who had

French soldier, his rat catcher dog and a large number of dead rats.

nowhere to hide within their trenches during such attacks. What chance an animal would have had, surviving in such circumstances, can only be guessed at.

As can be seen from the above photograph, a French soldier has used his dog to try and rid the trenches of the rats that he and his colleagues had to live with. There are well over 100 rats in that photograph, which the dog would have caught in a relatively small area of ground. Although both cats and dogs were used to deal with rat infestations, dogs, especially terriers, were much more effective in killing rats.

In December 1915, in an effort try and deal with what had become a plague of almost epidemic proportion of rats, the French authorities sent a train load of some 2,700 terriers from Paris to the Western Front. They were the ideal dog for the situation, killing rodents is what they did. They were vastly different from cats in this respect. A cat would attack one rat at a time, even play with for a while, before killing it and slowly eating it. A terrier on the other hand would attack a group of rats, and quickly kill one at a time, each of the rodents usually dispatched with a single bite. They didn't stop to eat any of their prey, all the terriers had on their minds was to kill.

One would think the most obvious way to get rid of the rats would be to shoot them, but this was strictly forbidden for two reasons. Firstly, it was deemed to be a waste of vital ammunition that could be better used to shoot the enemy with, and secondly, it was dangerous. If part-deranged men started wantonly discharging their rifles aimlessly around their trenches, the chances of wounding or killing a nearby colleague would be pretty high.

To put the rat problem into perspective, just one male and female couple could produce as many as 900 offspring each year. That many from just one couple. Multiply that by thousands of pairs and you quickly get the idea of just how bad the problem was.

The rats' presence greatly increased the chances of soldiers becoming ill. Weil's disease was an infection soldiers could catch by coming into contact with infected animal urine, usually in the dirty water that constantly lay about in the bottom of their trenches. Any cuts or scratches the soldiers had, especially on their feet or lower legs, could easily be the source of any subsequent infection. Weil's disease can also enter the human body through the nose, mouth or eyes, and can be fatal, although not always.

Chapter 6

Dogs

At the beginning of the First World War, Germany had several thousand dogs as part of its military might, whilst Britain, on the other hand, had just one. Why the disparity isn't clear, but an immediate observation would be that the British Army had never seen a military use for them up to that point in time, other than being a regimental mascot.

It was Lieutenant Colonel Edwin Hautenville Richardson, of the British Army, who had the foresight to press for the use of dogs on the Western Front, but that didn't happen via the British Army until 1917. He had been involved with dogs for most of his life. They had always intrigued him as pets but he saw their potential as working dogs.

Dogs and handlers at their kennels.

He had read up on how dogs had been used centuries before, by military generals in both the ancient Greek and Roman armies. The French, under Napoleon and in the years leading up to the First World War, and some European armies, were also using dogs for military purposes, but Britain wasn't one of them.

After retiring from the army in 1894, he moved up to Scotland where he trained dogs with his wife Blanche. In 1905, Richardson was contacted by the Russian Embassy in London, who wanted his assistance in the form of supplying them with a number of 'ambulance dogs', for their war with Japan in the Russo–Japanese war. He agreed to help with the Russians' request. He sent them several Airedales, all of whom performed admirably.

He was also contacted by Major General Tucker, who was the commanding officer of British forces in Scotland. There was an impending troop review at Edinburgh, before King Edward VII, and Richardson was invited to take part in the review with his ambulance dogs. He readily agreed and did not disappoint. Dressed in eye-catching Red Cross dog coats, the four young collies he took with him performed exactly as they had been trained to do.

Major General Tucker had not only been impressed with Richardson and the high level to which he trained his dogs, but also the dogs themselves, and what they brought to the table in a military sense. It had been apparent on many issues that some senior army officers and individuals in the War Office were living so far in the past that they were blind to the problems being faced. There had been no real appreciation of nurses and the effectiveness of what they could achieve, even going as far as turning down offers from individuals and groups who were offering their services for free to go and work on the Western Front. The true benefits of aircraft as offensive military weapons had been totally overlooked, with many only seeing them as an observation platform at best.

With most senior officers in the British Army coming from cavalry backgrounds, many of them still felt that full-on cavalry charges were the way to go, seeming not to appreciate that military tactics, as well as the effectiveness of weaponry, had progressed since the 1880s. How a group of men and horses, charging head-on towards a line of enemy machine guns that were spewing out round after round of bullets at a rapid rate of knots, was still felt to be a sound military tactic, beggared belief.

Dogs had become just another example of the War Office's apparent ineptitude and lack of forward thinking, which was highlighted even more as many other countries, having already realised their usefulness in time of war, had already developed their own dog training facilities for military purposes.

In an attempt at persuading the War Office of the usefulness and effectiveness of dogs in a military sense, Tucker sent them the following report:

> Forwarded and strongly recommended.
>
> Seeing that every foreign government has already recognised the use of dogs, either for ambulance purposes or sentry work, or both, I am of the opinion that advantage should be taken without delay of Major E H. Richardson's knowledge and experience in the matter of breeding and training of them, and some military training centre selected for the purpose. It seems like Salisbury Plain might offer greater facilities in this respect than Aldershot; but on his point, as on other matters of details, I suggest that Major Richardson be consulted.

With the benefit of hindsight, there was a certain element of irony attached to the next request for Richardson's assistance in dog-related matters. In 1907, he was asked to attend the Turkish Embassy in London. The reason behind the request was that the Turkish ruler, Sultan Abdul Hamid, who kept a large harem of women at his palace in Yildiz Kiosy, believed that a number of unknown men had been attempting to gain entry to his palace. The request from the sultan was that he took some of his dogs to the royal palace and show his servants, along with some of his army officers, how they should be used to prevent any further breaches of palace security.

During the seven years leading up to the beginning of the First World War, Richardson and his skill and knowledge of training dogs for military purposes was in great demand across Europe. In 1908, a somewhat complicated correspondence saw Richardson supplying tracking dogs, to be used for medical purposes, for the Spanish Army, who were fighting in Morocco at the time. The request wasn't a direct approach from the Spanish authorities though. Instead it came from the Empress Eugenie of Bulgaria. The connection between the two countries was that the Queen of Spain was the god-daughter of the Empress Eugenie.

The Abor Expedition was a punitive one, instigated against the Abors in Assam, which is situated on the north-eastern frontier of India. The expedition took place between October 1911 and April 1912, and followed the murder of the assistant political officer of the Sadiya and Lakhimpur districts, Mr Noel Williamson. This resulted in Richardson once again being called upon to help out. It was the Gurkhas who asked him to bring over dogs for use as sentries.

Richardson's skill and ability was starting to be recognised on a global scale. It seemed to be that no matter where in the world an armed conflict was going on, and one of the warring factions considered the use of dogs in some capacity, it was Richardson they turned to.

In 1911, the Italians, who were fighting the Turkish in Tripoli, were using dogs with their ambulance teams and as sentries. Once again, it was Richardson who was in charge of the dogs. Once back in the UK he was asked by different regiments of the British Army to send them some of his dogs, so that the men of these regiments could undertake training with them. Richardson duly obliged. One of these was the Norfolk Regiment.

In 1914, but before the outbreak of war, Richardson was invited to Russia, but on this occasion there was no request for him to bring his dogs. So high was his international reputation in the training of dogs for military purposes, the Russians wanted him to judge the Military and Police Dog Trials in Semenoff.

Richardson used many different dogs, including Bloodhounds, Airedales, and Collies, but he was equally adept at deciding on which dogs suited each of the disciplines.

What was truly amazing in relation to Richardson and his dogs was the report that Major General Tucker, who had recognised their usefulness, had sent to the War Office during the early years of the century. Despite his strongest possible suggestion and recommendation, they had not deemed it necessary for dogs to become an additional tool for the British Army, so had not moved forward on Tucker's report. After the war had already begun in August 1914, Richardson offered his services and those of his dogs to the War Office. All he received in return was a stony silence, so he returned to training his dogs with a hope that official attitudes would change, which they eventually did, but this only appears to have come about after repeated requests for dogs from

British Army officers serving on the Western Front. He did, however, receive a positive response from the British Red Cross, and travelled out to Belgium with some trained ambulance dogs, but he arrived in Brussels at exactly the same time as German forces, so rather than wait to be captured and taken prisoner, he immediately left with his dogs and returned to England via Ostend.

In October 1914, Major Richardson wrote an article, which appeared in the *Boy's Own Paper*, about his approach to training dogs for military and police purposes. He started by explaining that many great generals from the past had recognised the benefits of using dogs for military purposes.

> Caesar used dogs to guard his camps; Frederick the Great caused his sentries to use them, Napoleon wrote about military watch-dogs; they were used in the Civil War of North and South America, as sentries and for tracking, also in the Russo-Turkish war of 1878. During the Franco-German war they were employed with great success. But only recently has the subject received really scientific attention.

Major Richardson then went on to outline the three different areas where he felt dogs could be usefully deployed, one of which was scouting and sentry duty.

> Scout dogs are particularly valuable at night, for with the descent of darkness, which renders the soldier himself so helpless, the hearing or scenting powers of the dog become most acute. He will hear or scent the stealthy approach of the enemy's patrols long before the sentry is aware of there being anybody in the neighbourhood. After hundreds of experiments, I have proved that a dog can hear 200 to 400 yards farther than a man; when wind or atmosphere is especially favourable for scenting, detection will come at far greater distances.
>
> Ambulance dogs search for wounded men after a battle. They go out ahead, or on long leads, with the searchers and stretcher bearers, and are of the greatest assistance in finding the wounded.

Messenger Dog carrying telephone line.

Doing duty as a messenger or ammunition dog is the most difficult thing of all to teach, and my experience is that of twenty or more likely-looking dogs, only one will prove to be worth training. But once properly educated, they are invaluable. In the Boxer Expedition, the German artillery had some of these dogs, and when it became necessary to shell a Chinese patrol, the orders were brought five miles by a dog in quick time; the dog was standing quietly by when the guns galloped up. For carrying ammunition to the firing line, dogs are of the utmost service. The most suitable breed of dog for such work that we have in this country is the Airedale. He is faithful and intelligent, and possesses all the qualities of scenting and hearing that are required.

Major Richardson must have felt that he was banging his head against a brick wall at the outbreak of the war, especially where those at the War Office were concerned, as it appeared that nobody listened, or wanted to listen to him on the matter of dogs and their usefulness to the nation's military cause.

But he didn't let this deter him from doing what he had to do to make himself heard. He knew the benefits that dogs could bring to fighting on the Western Front, especially with the stalemate of trench warfare. Other countries had been using dogs for different military purposes for years, and to great effect. Germany was one of these nations. At the beginning of the war, Germany had an incredible 6,000 trained dogs at its disposal, many of which were used as sentries. Russia was employing her dogs in the same way.

The natural instinct of these dogs was to give warning of an approaching danger, and as both countries had been using dogs in this capacity for many years, they had an enormous advantage over any other armies in the matter of detecting night attacks on their lines at the earliest possible moment. The Germans valued so highly the role of the sentry dog that in every town they seized since the start of the war, one of their first acts was to capture all dogs likely to be of use for this work, and to destroy all other dogs that were of no use to them, so as to reduce the number available to the Allies when they eventually retook the town or village.

In spite of all this available information, both the British and French War Offices continued to be sceptical of the ability of dogs for any work other than that related to ambulance work, despite the fact that the absence of watchdogs from their armoury proved to be somewhat of a handicap to Allied units.

Despite no official support or backing from the War Office, Major Richardson had sent out fully trained 'sentry' dogs to about thirty different battalions of the British Expeditionary Force. This came about as a result of the commanding officers of the regiments concerned making direct contact with Major Richardson. They took this course of action after their direct appeals to the War Office failed to elicit any response.

Major Richardson added that he had already received positive reports back from some of the commanding officers about the standard of work that the dogs had provided to the soldiers on the ground.

The Allied nation of Belgium even employed dogs to carry light machine guns, as well as employing a number of dogs in ambulance work, where they helped identify wounded soldiers on the battlefield.

In early June 1915, it was reported that the authorities had taken the decision to jointly charge Major Richardson and the *Times* newspaper, under the restrictions of the Defence of the Realm Act, with publishing information which might be useful to the enemy.

The matter was heard at the Mansion House Police Court on Saturday, 5 June 1915, when the summons against Major Richardson and the *Times* newspaper was dismissed by the court.

The summons came about as the result of a letter written by Major Richardson and published by the *Times* newspaper on 21 May 1915, headed, '*The need for compulsion*' and which contained the following passage:

> The last of the French reserves are out, and at the present moment young raw recruits are being called up.

As at the previous hearing on the matter, the Treasury, which was the department that had issued the summons in the first place, was represented by Mr Bodkin. The *Times Publishing Company* was represented by Mr Gordon Hewart, KC, and Mr W. Frampton and Mr Bland, the publisher, and Mr H. C. Macardie, represented Major Richardson.

Major Radcliffe, from the War Office, was recalled and cross-examined by Mr Gordon Hewart. He told the court that he gave evidence partly as an expert in military matters. He was aware that in August 1914, a general mobilisation order was issued by the French military authorities, and that order was published in a most conspicuous way throughout the Empire.

Mr Hewart, in reply to the magistrate, said he proposed to show that this order contained all the information which was conveyed in the letter written by Major Richardson, and was freely commented upon by the leading papers in Germany. That order was published as long ago as 2 August 1914, whereas the letter in question, the one written by Major Richardson, wasn't penned until 18 May 1915. The Lord Mayor pointed out to Mr Hewart that the letter said, 'at the present moment raw recruits are being called out', and if that be the case it surely meant the process had just begun. Mr Hewart pointed out to the Lord Mayor that the process had in fact been going on for a period of seven weeks, and had been reported upon in the French Senate, and commented upon in well-known German newspapers.

Mr Bodkin, who was representing the Treasury, submitted that anything which took place in the French Senate was immaterial to the enquiry, and the witness could not be cross-examined on it. He continued by saying that the letter written by Major Richardson had to be considered in its entirety, and that as it included, 'Young lads in their teens are going to the firing line', such a statement at that time was a matter of great importance for Germany to know. It wasn't referring to how things were a couple of months earlier, it was talking about how they were there and then. The comments were an intimation from an eye-witness at the French front, and that young and raw youths were being called up to face the enemy in the front line trenches on 21 May 1915, a time and location where Major Richardson was on that very day. That was as clear a case of providing information to the enemy that they would be fighting against very inexperienced troops that he had ever heard of.

Mr Frampton said that the defence could not accept Major Radcliffe as an expert witness on the construction of a document. In further cross-examination he said he was aware that under the general mobilisation order, recruits of 20 years of age would be called to the colours in 1914. The order had been commented on by a host of German newspapers, including the *Cologne Gazette*, and in addition the *Reuters* news agency also printed the same information. Mr Hewart further added that whatever had been printed in whichever publication, all of the information that any of them had reported on had first been approved and passed by the French Bureau, therefore it made a mockery of the suggestion that either the *Times* newspaper or Major Richardson had been guilty of any offence of publishing information which might be useful to the enemy.

The content of Major Richardson's letter and what it actually constituted, was argued and re-argued by both sides. It certainly appeared that for whatever reason, the British establishment, or part of it, were trying their hardest to discredit Major Richardson and cast a lingering shadow over his good name. The prosecution even lamenting the fact that in signing the letter, E.H. Richardson, Major, it increased its importance, as it purported to be a military opinion. The fact that Major Richardson had retired from the army some 20 years earlier, information that would have been known by Germany and France for that matter, appeared to be lost on the prosecution.

In closing, Mr Hewart stated that the prosecution had been deplorable, ill-advised and an injurious mistake, made even more confusing by the knowledge that the French military authorities had not, and did not, support the prosecution, which beggars the question, why the matter had ever been prosecuted in the first place.

The matter had first be heard at the same court on Monday, 31 May 1915, in response to a letter written by Major Richardson dated Friday, 21 May. During that hearing it was clearly stated that the French military authorities contacted the War Office and complained of the publication of the letter in the strongest possible terms. It is strange that just five days later the same French authorities were distancing themselves from those comments. So the question remains as to who was behind the original decision to prosecute Major Richardson.

As he first highlighted when spoken to by the police on the matter, he expected everything that he had written to have been checked by the official censor, so when it appeared in the *Times* newspaper, as he had written it, he just naturally assumed that there was no problem with what he had written.

Major Richardson's name appeared in the news once more during the course of 1915, but not because he had been prosecuted again by the British authorities, or because of anything to do with his dog training skills and abilities, but because of the death of his youngest son, Second Lieutenant Angus Macdonald Richardson, who was only 18 years of age and serving with the 2nd Battalion, Gordon Highlanders. He was killed in action on Saturday, 25 September 1915, the first day of the Battle of Loos. He has no known grave but his name is commemorated on the Loos Memorial, which is situated in the Pas de Calais region of France.

Eventually the War Office did contact Richardson, asking him to set up a British War Dog Training School, but remarkably they didn't do this until 1917, nearly three years into the war. During this time Richardson carried on training his dogs at his home at Carnoustie in Scotland. He focused on teaching them how to find wounded soldiers on the battlefield, being messenger dogs, and on having them perform as sentries. Messenger dogs were usually of the smaller breed, such as collies, sheepdogs, retrievers or lurchers, as by the nature of the work they were being used for, they had to be able to travel as fast as possible. The dogs used for sentry duty were usually from the larger breed of dogs, such as Great Danes, Bull Mastiffs or St Bernards.

The chosen location for the school was the Artillery Barracks at Shoeburyness in Essex. Richardson initially used animals he deemed suitable for training from establishments such as Battersea Dogs' Home, but as the demand grew for more and more dogs from officers serving on the Western Front, another strategy was required. An appeal was made to

Clock Tower at Horseshoe Barracks, Shoeburyness.

Parade Square at Horseshoe Barracks, Shoeburyness.

the general public asking them to donate their pet dogs. In 1918, the War Dog Training School, having outgrown its home at Shoeburyness, moved to the Matley Ridge Camp at Lyndhurst, New Forest, Hampshire, after the Trench Mortar School closed and moved from the camp. Richardson, his men, and some 200 dogs moved into the camp, and simply picked up where they had left off at Shoeburyness. This wouldn't be the last home of the War Dog Training School; that was at the massive army camp at

Bulford on Salisbury Plain. When the war finished and before the school was closed and the dogs found new homes, they were used to assist the camp's guards and sentries. The camp was also home to German POWs, as well as large amounts of excess war-time equipment.

When the dogs and their keepers arrived in France they first went to a reception area at the main Etaples base, situated on the French coast. The rule of thumb was one keeper was responsible for, and looked after, a maximum of three dogs. At any given time there could be as many as 800 dogs being kept in kennels at Etaples. Although to each of the keepers, the dogs had individual names, such as Paddy, Jack and Champion, to everybody else they were simply known by the number on their collar. This was to try and stop soldiers on the front line from getting too attached to them, as many of them were killed in action. Losing a comrade could be painful enough for a soldier to deal with, so losing a dog that reminded them of home, or of their life before the war, wasn't seen by the military authorities as a positive experience.

When the animals and their keepers were sent from Étaples to their allocated brigade, the keeper always remained at the brigade headquarters, which is where all messages came into. There was a strict rule for the dogs not to be petted, and under no circumstances were they to be fed by the troops, they were handed over to their keepers. This was extremely difficult for a group of men, on foreign soil, separated from their loved ones, and from a nation of dog lovers. Add to this the fact that they did not know if they would even be alive at the end of the day. There was a sound reason for this, which was that the dogs needed to stay focused, because they knew that once they reached their destination they would be met by their keeper and fed. The rules were that a dog should not be kept in front line trenches for longer than twelve hours, this was in line with the dog being fed, as most dogs can go for twelve hours without eating. The twelve-hour rule was to ensure that they didn't get to a stage where they became over hungry, which might then affect their performance, and determine whether they reached their destination with their important message, or were killed en route.

Another sad aspect of the war was the lack of forward thinking by the War Office in relation to the use of dogs for military purposes, especially as most other countries across Europe, were well ahead of the game, with their soldiers having trained with dogs for years before the war had even begun. The sadness came in the large numbers of dogs who had been put down, mainly because of food shortages. Most of these were young, fit and healthy, many of which would have been suitable for training as military dogs.

By October 1915, Major Richardson had fully trained and sent no fewer than 132 dogs for use by British forces on the Western Front. It is often said that a man's best friend is his dog, and during the First World War, no other dog proved this to be the case better than the Airedale Terrier. There were many occasions when they discovered and helped recover a wounded soldier in peril and distress, putting into practice the almost instinctive canine faculty to protect and rescue. The Germans were so far ahead of the British and Allies when it came to the use of dogs. By October 1915, Germany had more than 2,000 dogs of different types working on the Western Front, who had already been recorded as having saved the lives of many German soldiers, who would have otherwise endured a very lonely and possibly painful demise.

Besides the dogs trained by Major Richardson for direct military purposes such as sentry duty, ambulance work and the sending of messages, they also played an important role as regimental mascots, for many British regiments, as well as many sides that were involved in the conflict. Some of these mascots came about in the shape of a prized gift, as was the case of the Royal West Kent Regiment, whose mascot was a Russian wolfhound, presented to them by Czar Nicholas II of Russia. Such dogs performed a much more important role than just that of an animal who stood correctly to attention on parade. They provided men with comfort and a feeling of wellbeing during their time at the front, which for many consisted of trauma and a dark cloud constantly hanging over them, which made for a painful experience. The presence of a dog that was happy to see them and responded by wagging its tail, and offering its paw in friendship, was a great help to many young men who were homesick and otherwise devoid of love and affection. Remember, many of these young men had never even left their villages before they enlisted in the army.

By July 1915, the French had made great inroads in the use of dogs for military purposes. The earlier uncertainty of their worth, by the French War Office, had been overcome and reconciled. They had particularly shown their worth in the area of finding and succouring wounded French soldiers, who otherwise might have died. The French experimented with four different methods. The dogs were originally trained to lay beside the wounded soldier they had discovered, and bark. This was fraught with danger, as besides notifying the French where their wounded comrade was, it also let the Germans know where he was as well. This in turn placed those sent forward to rescue the wounded soldier in grave danger from German snipers. Method number two consisted of the dog being trained to locate a wounded soldier and bring back his Kepi. The dangers here revolved around the 'what if' scenario. The assumption was that a wounded soldier would more than likely have his Kepi fall from his head, which was helpful if that's what happened, but if the Kepi had remained in place, due to the wearing of the chin strap, there was the real risk that the dog, in an effort to remove it from the soldier's head, would end up accidentally biting the man. The next idea was to attach a 'slide' to the dogs collar, in which was placed a strip of cotton which the wounded man would then unclip from the dog when he had been discovered. What the man was then supposed to do with his new found strip of cotton and how that helped him exactly, is unclear. This system pre-supposed that the located wounded soldier was conscious.

After many experiments with the different variations, it was decided to go with a combination of the last three options. Only dogs that were deemed to be gentle enough were used, and the training was honed to such a degree that the dogs were even trained to try and remove a wounded soldier's Kepi, but only if he hadn't secured it to his head with his chin strap. Each dog was also given the strip of cotton for the wounded soldier to take. If the dog subsequently returned without a Kepi and the strip of cotton, it was deduced that the wounded man had been able to use the latter; should the dog return with a Kepi and the cloth strip it would be assumed that the wounded man was unconscious, and the dog was then attached to a leash so that he could lead the hospital orderly to him. The orderly would then carry out basic first aid, before removing him to the nearest aid post.

The dogs were also trained to act as orderlies, a role which they carried out to a very high standard. They were each issued with a hollow collar into which a message could be inserted, and also trained to reconnoitring patrols, as well as supporting them. These dogs were trained to maintain communication between pickets and their sentries. To be able to undertake this role they were taught to go from one handler to another, initially over short distances, which were gradually increased up to a distance of 5 miles. Once they had mastered that particular skill, the dogs were then trained to go to different places, with the assistance of different handlers who used special signals, in areas that were unfamiliar to them.

By 1915, the French had already trained vast numbers of dogs to undertake numerous different roles that greatly assisted their soldiers serving along the miles and miles of the Western Front. Some of the larger dogs were harnessed to small wooden carts, and helped carry provisions, ammunition, and various pieces of equipment to the front line trenches.

Some interesting information about the German use of dogs for military purposes came to light in July 1915, although it had been written in March 1915, by Dr Humbert, who at the time was in charge of the hospital at Bussang. He wrote a piece in the monthly bulletin of the Saint Hubert Club de France.

Ever since German military authorities took the decision to attach a team of dogs to each *Jager* (Rifle) battalion, the use and deployment of dogs in the German Army steadily increased. This was due to the close cooperation between the German military authorities, and the people in charge of most of the national dog associations. Foremost in this respect was the *Verein for Feutsche Schaferhunde* (German Sheepdog Club), which had been founded in 1889, and which by 1915 had more than 4,000 members. Its stud books contained somewhere in the region of 45,000 entries and a special register in the case of German military mobilisation. Each entry included whether the sheepdog in question was deemed suitable to be trained, or had already been trained, for police duties, ambulance work, patrol work or domestic duties. It was estimated at the time that about 4,000 of the sheep dogs were included in the special register.

It would be worth noting at this stage that the British War Office had not made contact with, or had any such plan in place with any of the British National Dog Associations. It would be another two years before they even gave official support to Major Richardson and requested him to set up a dog training school for the British Army. The War Office were so far behind what the French, Belgian and German military already had in place, not only was it embarrassing, it showed just how inept and how backward thinking those who worked within the War Office actually were.

A good example of where Britain was with her military dog training situation was clearly displayed in Coventry on 9 July 1915. The city's magistrates' court had several dog-related cases before them, but not for cruelty to animals, not even for theft of dogs. The offences being dealt with were for keeping a dog without a licence. Two men who lived in Carmelite Road, Coventry, but not at the same address, Mr Ernest Thompson and Mr Oliver Chatland, were both found guilty of that same offence and were fined 9 shillings each. Another man, Mr Mark Wood of 45 Gosford Street, Coventry, was also fined 9 shillings for a similar offence, but his wife came up with an absolutely brilliant piece of mitigation, by telling the court that the dog didn't belong to her husband. He had supposedly sold it three weeks earlier, but despite this, the dog repeatedly returned to their home.

The following British dog-related story has a slightly different outcome, and is one that couldn't help but bring a smile to one's face. In the early months of the war, a loving little dog who had somehow acquired the unfortunate name of Ugly, arrived in France. Not as one might think, an official, well-groomed military dog of the British Army, but as an unowned, scruffy and unkempt-looking mongrel. He had been a stowaway on a Channel Packet. If his scars and scratches were anything to go by, he had certainly been used to fighting, that was for sure.

He became attached to the Army Service Corps (Pickford's Light Horse) and his allotted duties were simply referred to as 'BX', which meant any sort of job that was going at the base; 'B' standing for base, and 'X' being the recognised algebraic symbol which signified an unknown quantity. He was first tasked to deal with what had become a severe problem at the docks, where rats had taken it upon themselves to savage the bales of hay waiting to be distributed to the relevant units as horse feed.

So successful was he at reducing the rats' numbers that he was rewarded with a promotion to the rank of corporal and double rations, jam being his utmost favourite of things that he liked to eat. He found himself in several fights with stray French dogs who had wandered into his newly acquired territory, which he wasn't about to give up so readily. In fact, Ugly had gained such a reputation for his fighting prowess, it had come to the notice of men fighting in the front line trenches. It had also been mentioned in polite conversation at the GHQ. Ugly had become quite the celebrity. One morning a dust-covered driver from the ASC pulled up in his vehicle amid the shell-strewn debris that was the dock area. The driver sought out an officer, and on finding a young lieutenant, he quickly handed him a package, and politely demanded a speedy response. The message contained within the envelope read as follows:

> Dug-out 68b, Battersea Rise, Tuesday.
>
> We always congratulated ourselves here in having the ugliest dog and the fiercest fighter in Flanders. We hereby challenge Corporal Ugly, ASC, to meet Sergeant Smiler, GHQ, to fight 25 rounds, catch as catch can, at any handy spot within or without the meaning of the Act. Stakes £5 a side, money down.

Inquiries were immediately made as to the standing, skill and fighting weight of Sergeant Smiler, and these being considered satisfactory, the challenge was accepted and Ugly was put into strict training, much to his disgust. His ration of jam was reduced, and he was put on an exclusive diet of bully beef and biscuit to harden his teeth and augment his angry passions. After a couple of quickly arranged rehearsals, albeit with a poodle and a wolfhound, it was readily agreed that his anger and passion had definitely been augmented. Both animals received treatment at a nearby medical clearing station.

A heavy book was made on the fight, and when the eagerly anticipated evening of the doggy duel finally arrived, the selected location was packed with a keen and expectant crowd. Sergeant Smiler duly arrived on time, carried triumphantly into the arena in a very large wooden Huntley & Palmer biscuit box, marked 'Ginger Nut', which contained a sufficiently large number of perforations for him to be able to safely breathe.

Ugly was ready and waiting, striding up and down like an expectant father showing everybody present that he was the daddy. By now, both dogs had caught each other's scents and the growling and gnashing of teeth began. He was supremely fit, a look that was matched only by his aggressive demeanour. So impressive in fact, that the betting had already opened at two to one on Ugly, even before his opponent had even been seen.

Sergeant Smiler, inside his wooden box marked 'Ginger Nut', was placed on the floor of the fight arena. The ties were undone, the lid raised and a side of the wooden box ripped open by a brave young Tommy, who quickly leapt backwards over the parapet of the arena. No sooner had he made it to safety, than the two dogs were engaged in their own interpretation of a Mexican stand-off.

Ugly began his routine first, like a Sumo wrestler, preparing to do battle. With his back hair bristling he crouched as if ready to spring into action, teeth bared and gums raised, as he psyched himself up, ready for the attack. But then, the unthinkable happened, he sat down, smiled and wagged his tail. As he glanced across at his opponent, he was confronted with his complete double, in size, shape and colour. Sergeant Smiler also crouched, lying on the ground as if he was frozen to the spot. Both dogs stared at each other quizzically, each recognising the other. There was no snarling or gnashing of teeth, just heavy breathing and playfulness, as the gathered soldiers waited with bated breath, waiting for the expected battle to commence. Without warning, the dogs launched at each other, but there was no biting and scratching, just joyful tail wagging and excited yaps as they tussled and mouthed each other's necks.

It was evident to all present that despite their bets and wishes, there was to be no fight, not even a bite or a scratch. It was more like a love-in as two long lost friends met for the first time in years. As it turned out Corporal Ugly and Sergeant Smiler were brothers from the same litter, separated as puppies, who had pursued different paths, only to meet up again on the Western Front in war-time France.

Truth is sometimes stranger than fiction, and despite any doubts you might have about the authenticity of this story, it is in fact true. A story that was responsible for bringing a smile to many a young British soldier's face, as they used whatever means that they had to get through their time in the trenches. Many told and retold the story over the years, and regardless of whether they were believed or not, they knew the truth, and to them, that was all that mattered.

The register of dogs kept by the Germans was meticulously maintained, and included information from not only the German Sheepdog Club but also the German Club for Ambulance Dogs. As the name of the latter club suggests, it specialised in the breeding and training of dogs that had been identified as being suitable for the discipline of retrieving wounded soldiers from the battlefield.

The dogs kept by the members of these two societies formed the reserve of the canine units for the German Army and their owners were informed shortly before mobilisation to keep them in readiness for requisition by the army.

Whilst the *Jager* battalions specialised in the deployment of dogs for patrol and sentry duty, dogs were employed by other regiments as well, with up to ten dogs being attached to each battalion.

The ambulance detachments, which formed part of each German regiment, generally had four ambulance dogs that were taken out at the same time as the stretcher-bearers were sent out. The breed used by the German Army referred to as the German Sheepdog, actually came from Alsace and Switzerland. Other breeds included the Doberman pinscher, the Airedale terrier and the boxer, as well as the Rottweiler, which was more readily used as a cattle dog.

It is absolutely astonishing to learn how two nations were at such different ends of the spectrum when it came to the subject of dogs in the military. What is most disturbing was not how well-advanced the Germans were in their planning and preparation in relation to dogs, but that at the exact same time, the British hadn't even begun to think about the use of dogs for military purposes. The War Office owed an enormous debt of gratitude to Major Richardson for his work in the training of dogs, which he had been carrying out for many years. At least when they eventually took their heads out of the sand and finally addressed the issue, it didn't take the UK years to start producing sufficient numbers of dogs to fulfil the roles that they were needed for.

It is sad to think that an estimated 1 million dogs died during the course of the First World War.

The Belgian Army often attached small wheeled carts to some of their dogs so that they could carry small amounts of supplies with them.

The War Office released a brief statement on 27 September 1915, in relation to military operations in Gallipoli.

> During the night of the 24th the Turks let loose watch dogs against French patrols. The dogs were all shot.

The outcome of such an attack must have been blatantly obvious, long before it was undertaken. It was just nothing more than a complete waste of animals' lives. What the Turks actually thought that they were going to achieve by such an action is unclear, but it was futile. Even a large dog who has been trained to attack is not going to fight its way past a well-aimed bullet or bayonet.

One of the more unusual dog stories from the First World War was about a Boston bull terrier named Sergeant Stubby. He was the only dog to be promoted to the rank of sergeant as a result of his exploits in combat, and he was also highly decorated for his feats. Sergeant Stubby was an American dog, which could cause one to question if such an accolade would have been bestowed upon him if he had been from any other country.

Stubby had started out as the mascot to the 102nd Infantry, 26th Yankee Division, and ended up becoming a fully-fledged combat dog. Whilst in front-line trenches he was injured in a German gas attack, which resulted in him being acutely sensitive to gas. This new found gift allowed Stubby to warn soldiers of an impending gas attack, which he did by running about and barking. They soon understood what he was telling them. He certainly was a very special dog and located many wounded American soldiers who had been left in no man's land. During his time on the Western Front he was wounded twice.

Sergeant Stubby.

Chapter 7

Cats

Cats were used extensively by both the British Army and the Royal Navy during the course of the First World War. It is estimated that half-a-million cats were shipped across the English Channel or served on board vessels of the Royal Navy. Ships had traditionally had cats as part of their crews going back hundreds of years. But they weren't on board to be pets for the crew to stroke anytime they were having a bad day, although I am certain that was a function which they did fulfil. Their main purpose was to rid the ship of vermin, which always somehow managed to get on board. If cats didn't keep the numbers down, there was a real chance of ships being overrun with mice and rats, who would eat into their food supplies, chew through ropes, and there was even the possibility that they would spread disease. Cats were also believed to be lucky.

The story goes that during the Crimea War in 1854, when the Russian town of Sevastopol was under siege by forces of the British, French and Ottoman

Sailor with two of the ships cats.

Cat aboard ship walking along a gun barrel.

Empires, a cat discovered much needed caches of food that had been supposedly hidden by the Russians before they had retreated inside the town's citadel. The cat then acquired the pet name of Crimean Tom, he was adopted by the British Army as an unofficial mascot and when the troops left for home after the fighting had finished he went with them.

On Saturday, 30 October 1914, the government hospital ship, the *Rohilla*, ran aground on rocks off the coast of Whitby. Initially, about sixty men who had been on board the vessel were rescued, but that left a further fifty men still on board. Some of them, rather than waiting to be rescued, decided to dive and jump into the waves of the turbulent seas, and swim the short distance to shore. Some reached the beach safely, albeit in an exhausted state, but others were not so fortunate, and their lifeless bodies were washed ashore.

At about noon, three men were seen to leave the boat, each floated on what appeared to be nothing more substantial than a wooden box. They were observed from the shore drifting slowly drifting towards Whitby Pier. In an attempt to intercept them, the Whitby lifeboat was launched from the beach, but the effort was in vain, and the three men were all lost.

At 4.30pm the Tyne motor lifeboat, the *Henry Vernon*, was launched in an attempt to reach the stricken vessel and rescue the remainder of those who were still on board the *Rohilla*. The twelve-man crew of the lifeboat fought their way slowly through the teeth of a heavy south-easterly gale, blinding showers of rain, and heavy seas to reach the vessel. The short journey took the lifeboat a staggering nine hours. The rescue of the remaining survivors began immediately, and fifty-one people were safely recovered onto the lifeboat, along with the somewhat bedraggled ship's cat. By 7.30am on Sunday morning the *Henry Vernon*, her twelve-man crew, the fifty-one survivors and the ship's cat, had all arrived safely at Whitby.

Out of 220 crew, nurses and patients on board the *Rohilla*, 143 were saved. Captain Nelson, who was in command of the ship, received the Bronze Medal of the Royal Society for the Prevention of Cruelty to Animals for the rescue of a kitten from the *Rohilla*.

In February 1915, the explorer, Sir Ernest Shackleton, who was on his Antarctic expedition, had reached South Georgia, 1,390 km south-east of the Falkland Islands. The main activity there was whaling, which employed around 300 men, all of whom were Norwegian. Whaling trawlers would go out with massive harpoon guns fitted to their boats, to catch their prey, which was brought back to the whaling station where the carcases would be cut up.

One of the most important members of the expedition's crew was Mrs Chippy, a dignified but somewhat ill-disciplined individual. The female in question was the ship's cat, who was brought aboard by the carpenter. Her favourite pastime was running up the rigging, and in this she was more agile than any man aboard. The members of the crew were extremely fond of the cat.

On Tuesday, 16 February 1915, the Spanish steamer *Antonia* ran aground at Cloughey Bay in County Down. Here the crew all managed to get off safely and were conveyed into Belfast. The captain and his twenty-three crew members, who were all Spanish nationals, were put up at the Sailors' Rest Home in Corporation Street, Belfast. Only one of the crew could speak English, and that was the boatswain, who on behalf of the entire crew was able to say thank you to the people of Cloughey for the kindness they had shown to him and his colleagues. The town was left with one memento of the occasion, this came in the form of the ship's cat, who had the presence of mind to jump in to the lifeboat when the crew were being rescued.

ANIMALS IN THE GREAT WAR

At 9am on Tuesday, 9 March 1915, SS *Princess Victoria* was torpedoed by a German submarine and sank about 20 miles off the Mersey Bar. During the summer season, she was usually engaged in trips around Scotland and some of the islands situated off the nation's west coast, with an average of around 200 passengers. Fortunately, when she sank, she was only carrying cargo from Aberdeen to Liverpool.

Captain John Cubbin and other members of his crew were subsequently interviewed about the incident, and all stated that they had lookouts positioned to actively seek out German submarines for the entire journey. By the time they saw the torpedo speeding towards them just below the surface, it was too late to change course and avoid the impact.

The weather was fine, and in keeping with what could be expected for the time of year. There was a fair amount of other shipping in the area, with the nearest vessel being only about 5 miles away from the *Princess Victoria.*

There was a massive explosion as the torpedo struck, and within ten minutes she had sunk beneath the waves, but due to the quick actions of the crew they were able to launch one of the ship's boats over the side which held the ship's captain and his twenty-three crew members, and managed to get far enough away from their sinking ship, so as not to get dragged under as she sank. A nearby minesweeper, whose crew had witnessed the sinking, quickly took the life boat in tow, and took her to the Liverpool Landing Stage. None of the crew were injured, but sadly, all three of the ship's cats were lost, all going down with the ship. Whether the cats were killed in the initial explosion, or could not be found in time to save them, is not known.

In March 2014, the National Archives released nearly 4,000 British Army unit War Diaries from the First World War. One particular entry, from July 1915, included a report that formed part of an intelligence briefing concerning a dog and two cats. It had been written by an officer of the 36th Brigade, which in turn was part of the Allied 12th Division.

The report about the animals contained just three lines.

> Two cats and a dog are under suspicion, as they have been in the habit of crossing our trenches at night; steps are being taken to trap them if possible.

Whether the report was in fact serious, or just some light-hearted way for the officer who wrote the report to try and make light of his stressful circumstances, isn't clear. What the report, or later entries, did not show was what the outcome of these observations was.

In January 1916, a train stopped at an unnamed south coast railway station, the door opened, and in stepped a sailor in his uniform. 'Come here Nigel,' the sailor called out, beckoning the cat on to the train. A slender-looking black cat gracefully crossed the gap between the platform and the carriage as the sailor sat down, taking up a window seat on the opposite side. The cat sprang nimbly up on to the long bench seat, then took six long steps, before curling up comfortably on the man's lap, purring loudly as he got into just the right position. One of the other passengers, looked at the sailor, and smiled. 'Ship's cat?' he enquired. 'That's exactly right,' the sailor replied with true naval brevity. The passenger leant forward to stroke the cat. 'Been chasing the Germans have you pussy?' he said. The sailor was pleased at the man's unsolicited admiration for his cat. 'We certainly have that Nigel, haven't we?' the sailor said, looking down lovingly at his pet, 'chasing around the North Sea after them. Caught one as well, didn't we Nigel? Now we are off home for a much-needed break. Then back after them again, eh, Nigel?'

In August 1917, a conference took place at the Anderton's Hotel in Fleet Street, London. The purpose of the conference was for seafarers of all grades to consider the crimes committed by the commanders and crews of German U-boats, against Allied shipping.

The SS *Belgian Prince*, a cargo ship, was attacked and sunk on 31 July 1917, by an unknown German U-boat, some 200 miles off the west coast of Ireland. The ship's crew had made it to their lifeboats, but they were caught by the surfacing U-boat, and were assembled on the hull of the submarine, and stripped of their life jackets. The submarine submerged and all but four of the *Belgian Prince's* crew drowned. One of the four who survived this act of cruelty by the Germans was Captain Henry Hassan, who was taken below decks of the U-boat before she submerged, never to be seen again.

Seaman George Seleski, a Russian sailor, and one of the three survivors of the *Belgian Prince*, read the following statement out at the conference.

I signed on at Liverpool on the 23rd July and sailed on the 24th. On July 31st, the ship was torpedoed without warning about 200 miles from the Irish coast. When the crew took to the boats the submarine hailed them to come alongside. They were then ordered to come on board the submarine. Five Germans who were in a small boat then smashed the lifeboat of the *Belgian Prince* with hatchets. The crew were then ordered to take off their lifebelts, and the lifebelts were taken down below in the submarine. The captain was ordered down below also.

The crew were on board the submarine for about an hour, on the foredeck, when without any warning, the submarine submerged and left the crew to swim about, there being nothing in sight except the *Belgian Prince*, which had not sunk, but we could only just see her in the distance. I then made up my mind to reach the ship, but I was endeavouring to save the third officer.

Mr Seleski's statement continued with him describing in great detail how he eventually made it back to the partly submerged *Belgian Prince*, but then had to avoid German sailors from the submarine that had attacked them, who had returned to the ship to remove the clothes from the officers' quarters. He described how to avoid being discovered he had to jump off the ship and hold on to its rudder whilst the German submarine opened fire on the *Belgian Princess* with her deck gun, in an effort to finish her off.

I then swam to a dinghy, which had floated off the ship, and after struggling for about half an hour, I managed to get into the boat, but prior to doing so I picked up the ship's cat, which had been floating about on a piece of timber from the ship, and placed it in the dingy. Thankfully it didn't struggle. After about half an hour I was picked up by a patrol boat, and when I got on board, the chief engineer and second were on board. I was then taken to Liverpool where we were landed, and I left the cat with the crew of the patrol boat.

It sounds like Mr Seleski and the ship's cat both had a very strong desire to survive, having been in the water from the time the lifeboats were lowered to when they were rescued by the patrol boat.

On Thursday, 27 June 1918, a story that was powerful enough to pull at the heart strings of animal lovers everywhere appeared in the pages of a Scottish daily newspaper. The article was written by Commander M.D. Evans of the Royal Navy.

About four months earlier he had been playing golf on the west coast of Scotland when he found a rabbits' nest, from which he picked out the three small baby rabbits that were, he guessed, only about a week old. He knew that one of the ship's cats had just produced her first litter of kittens, so rather than leave the defenceless baby rabbits to an uncertain future, he took them back to the ship with him. He lay the rabbits (also called kittens) in amongst the kittens. The cat took to them straight away, and her litter of four then became eight, although one rabbit subsequently died from eating carrots at too early an age. As the rabbits grew, they still saw the cat as their mother, and the cat still saw them as her kittens, and washed them every day.

Even during a time of war, it is often to animals that men turn, to bring back some humanity and humility into their lives.

Cats served three purposes in the army as well. They were despatched to the trenches on the Western Front to rid the walk ways of rats and mice. Reducing their numbers and keeping them down was an important matter for the authorities as it could help reduce disease and illness. Too many men were being killed and wounded by German bullets and bombs, so losing men to disease and illness was the last thing that was needed.

Young men who were away from their homes and loved ones, many for the first time, in some foreign clime, often found themselves out-of-sorts, lonely and pining for home. It was with this in mind that these same cats became surrogate companions and pets for the young men, which also reminded them of being back home. One can only guess at the terror these cats went through during enemy bombardments of the trenches they were in.

Sadly, there were also times when cats were sacrificed to save the lives of soldiers. They were used to detect the numerous gas attacks on Allied positions by the Germans, because the cuddly little feline bundles of fur were more susceptible to gas fumes than the soldiers were, and those few extra seconds could literally mean the difference between life and death for soldiers in the trenches.

Chapter 8

Camels

Like horses, camels, or ships of the desert, as they are also known, have been used in time of war for thousands of years. In the hotter and more rugged terrains they have been the cavalry of the Middle East and surrounding areas, where they have quite often been the animal of choice. That was still the case at the time of the First World War, for both the Allies and Ottoman Armies, who fought against each other, throughout the region.

Facts about Camels

The soldiers who rode camels were known as cameliers. After riding to their destinations, they would dismount and engage the enemy on foot as infantrymen. Once placed in the *barraked* position, where they are made to kneel down, camels tended to remain quite calm and docile. This allowed twelve to sixteen camels to be looked after by just one man whilst his colleagues went into battle. Since each company consisted of around 184 officers and men, each with a camel, once they had reached their destination it only required about eleven men to remain with, and tend to all the camels.

Imperial Camel Corps.

As well as being ridden, camels were also used to carry equipment, stores and ammunition. They were ideal animals to be used in desert terrain, and could go up to five days without the need to drink water, compared with a horse, which would require watering every day. A camel's walking pace is estimated to be about 3 miles per hour, a similar speed to a human's walking pace.

Although camels were by their very nature quite calm animals, they could also be extremely stubborn and aggressive, especially the males during the rutting season. This situation was exasperated somewhat as the beasts used by the Imperial Camel Corps were un-neutered. They were not against attacking humans, and when they did so it was with their teeth. If they managed to get a man on the ground, it was not uncommon for them to try and crush him, by pounding down on them with their knees.

Unlike horses that required grass (which wasn't that plentiful in desert regions), hay, or oats, to be able to sustain their strength, a camel could survive on the twigs of a tree or a bush, even thorny ones. This meant a camel could actually find and eat its food as it marched along, or during halts, with no need to bring a large supply of animal feedstuffs.

Imperial Camel Corps on patrol.

Having said that, camels were also perfectly at home eating chopped straw and grain. If a camel was provided with food in this way, it was placed on a cloth to prevent him from also accidentally eating sand and earth, which could cause colic.

Unlike horses, camels do not require shoeing, as they have pads on their feet rather than hoofs. This gave them the advantage of being adaptable to any surface, although their feet did need wrapping to protect against cuts and abrasions if they were traversing across rough and rocky ground. Boggy ground could be just as dangerous for them, as this could lead to them to slipping, and cause dislocation of their hind legs.

One thing camels and horses did have in common was their big teeth, large enough to deliver a very painful bite, which both were more than capable of giving.

For most of the war, each camel company was made up of four sections. Each section would consist of eight groups of four men, all armed with a standard British Army issue Lee Enfield .303 rifle, and a fifteen-man machine gun section, who would be responsible for maintaining and operating three Lewis guns. There were also eight signallers, a medical orderly, a veterinary sergeant, and a headquarters group, which totalled 184 officers and men.

The Imperial Camel Corps Brigade didn't come into existence until more than two years into the war, on 19 December 1916, under the command of Brigadier General Clement Leslie Smith VC MC. It included troops from Australia, Great Britain and New Zealand, as part of the Egyptian Expeditionary Force for service in the Middle East. One of the reasons for its formation was to fight against the Islamist Senussi tribe, who were supported by a number of Arab and Berber tribes who lived in the Libyan-Egyptian border region. During the latter months of 1915, the Senussi, with the backing and encouragement of the Ottoman Empire, had been attacking British and Egyptian border outposts, which up to that time had been noticeably devoid of any real British military presence, which was also quite possibly the reason that Senussi warriors were so agreeable to attack the isolated outposts.

Originally the brigade consisted of only three battalions; the 1st (Australian), 2nd (British) and 3rd Australian. The 4th (ANZAC) Battalion was formed in May 1917. Each of the four battalions contained 770 men and 922 camels.

Australian Camel Corps.

Many of the men who ended up being part of the Imperial Camel Corps had originally arrived in the region as replacements in such equine regiments as the New Zealand Mounted Rifles, the Australian Light Horse and the British Yeomanry Regiments. But so many replacements had been sent over from those countries, they could not sensibly be absorbed. Having recognised this, General Sir Archibald Murray, the British Commander of the Egyptian Expeditionary Force, agreed that excess men could be transferred to the Imperial Camel Corps, so that it could be strengthened and expanded in size. All it took was two months of input at the Camel Training Depot, which was situated at Abbassia, Cairo, and the men were ready to trot off into the desert seated astride their new-found companions. A lot of their day-to-day work was to carry out long-range desert patrols across the region of the Sinai desert, looking out for Ottoman forces.

They also had a number of support units, including the Hong Kong and Singapore (Mountain) Artillery Battery of the Royal Garrison Artillery, (but whose men were actually drawn from the British Indian Army), the 265th (Camel) Machine Gun Squadron, which used eight powerful Vickers heavy machine guns, a section of Royal Engineers, the 10th (Camel) Field Troop, the Australian (Camel) Field Ambulance, a Signal Section, the 97th Australian Dental Unit, which consisted of only four staff, and an ammunition column admin section. The brigade's camels were cared for by a Mobile Veterinary Section, as well as at the Camel Veterinary Hospital, also situated at the Remount and Training Depot at Abbassia. At its peak the brigade consisted of 4,150 officers and men and 4,800 camels. To begin with, Indian, also known as Bikaner, camels were used by the Imperial Camel Corps. These continued to be used throughout the war, but as the war progressed it was the Egyptian camels that were used for riding. This was because they were generally lighter, meaning they could travel faster. They didn't totally replace the Bikaner camels, as they were ideal for carrying heavy supplies and equipment.

To keep the men fresh, only three of the battalions were active at any given time, whilst the fourth would be rested and their equipment cleaned and replaced.

In August 1915, there was a lot of talk in both national and local British newspapers about camels. This was at a time where many people hadn't even heard of camels, let alone seen one. Most British people thought only of horses as animals that could be used for military purposes.

Here is one article which appeared in the *Framlingham Weekly News*. It was entitled *Camels in Warfare*.

> Troops in Egypt, and other places where sand is only too plentiful, use camels to a very large extent for transport purposes. They take the place of horses, indeed, in nearly all cases where horses are used in colder countries. Special rules are laid down in the Army regulations for dealing with camels, for they are far more difficult to handle than horses. Unless it is absolutely necessary, they are not allowed to march during the heat of the day, nor should they be kept loaded for more than four hours at a time. The rules lay it down that camels used for transportation should be allowed five or six hours a day to feed. The ordinary desert camel however, needs only to be watered once in three days. The desert animal, by the way is never groomed like a horse, but brushed down with a piece of sacking.
>
> Most people have the idea that the animal is very swift, though the contrary is actually the case. The rate of a baggage camel is, indeed, only two and a half miles an hour, and that of a trotting camel, five miles an hour.

In early July 1916, volunteers were called up to the Imperial Camel Corps from the different Yeomanry regiments stationed in Egypt. This time it was the turn of the Berkshire Yeomanry to swap their horses for camels, and the experience that came with it. At first their new mounts appeared not only slightly strange, but somewhat tame for what was not a very pretty, gangly looking animal. For the men it was a big change from what they were used to. The horses that they had become accustomed to as cavalry men were sleek and fast moving, whilst the camels were predominantly one-paced, at a speed more akin to a plod than a gallop.

Men of the Berkshire Yeomanry commented that the most noticeable difference between the two animals was how much easier it was for them to bond with their horses than it was with the camels. Where the horse was a noble beast, the camel was almost obstinate by comparison, and the men found them hard to form any kind of relationship with, which they found slightly unnerving. But the men knew that complaining and moaning about their new companions wasn't going to help them. The change was something that they had to deal with, and quickly, because to claim, as experienced horsemen, that they were unfamiliar with their newfound companions was like admitting they were ignorant, whereas to accept and embrace the change replaced the ignorance with knowledge, and allowed the riders to begin looking at their charges in a new and more positive light. The men of the Berkshire Yeomanry quickly came to realise that it didn't really matter whether they preferred to be riding horses or camels, but if they were going to operate in desert areas then the camel was far better suited to that particular terrain than a horse was.

The Battle of Romani took place between 3 and 5 August 1916 and began as a German attack on the Suez Canal, with fighting taking place near the Egyptian town of Romani. The Allied units involved in the fighting were the 52nd (Lowland) Division and the 4th Battalion, Imperial Camel Corps. But that wasn't the end of the matter as the 4th Battalion, mounted on their camels, chased after the joint Ottoman and German forces all the way to Bir el Abd.

Only a few days after the Imperial Camel Corps was established, the Battle of Magdhaba took place on 23 December 1916, during the Defence of Egypt section of the Sinai and Palestine Campaign. It was the brigade's first large engagement. The corps' 4th (ANZAC) Battalion engaged elements of the Ottoman Army, who were in entrenched

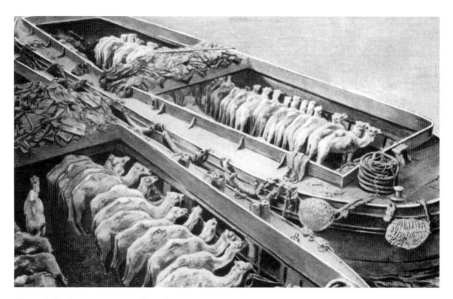

Camels being transported on barges.

defensive positions situated to the south and east of Bir Lahfan in the Sinai desert. The Allied forces won the day, forcing the Ottoman garrison to withdraw, and in doing so, securing the town of El Arish.

The Imperial Camel Corps Brigade was made up of the following sections and men. Although mentioned above, the following list breaks the different sections down into manpower levels.

Brigade Headquarters	40 men
1st (Australian) Camel Battalion	770 men
2nd (Imperial) Camel Battalion	770 men
3rd (Australian) Camel Battalion	770 men
4th (ANZAC) Camel Battalion	770 men

The following were the brigade's different support groups.

Hong Kong & Singapore (Mountain) Battery	255 men
265th (Camel) Machine Gun Squadron	115 men
10th (Camel) Field Troop, Royal Engineers	71 men
Signal Section	30 men
Australian (Camel) Field Ambulance	185 men
97th Australian Dental Unit	4 men

Mobile Veterinary Section	42 men
Brigade Ammunition Column	75 men
Brigade Train	245 men

By the end of the war, 67 members of the Imperial Camel Corps had died. A further 202 men who served with the Australian Imperial Camel Corps had also died, along with 45 members of the New Zealand Imperial Camel Corps.

The final remnants of the Imperial Camel Corps were the British companies. Those from Australia and New Zealand had been disbanded by the end of June 1918 and reverted to serving with mounted regiments. When the corps was finally disbanded in 1919, there were only two British companies left. Originally the camels were going to be transferred to the Camel Transport Corps, but after the intervention of Colonel T. E. Lawrence, better known in a historical sense as Lawrence of Arabia, the commander of the Egyptian Expeditionary Force, Lieutenant General Edmund Allenby, agreed that they would be better put to use by being given to the Arab Army.

In June 1917, aircraft of the Turkish air force bombed the 3rd Battalion's camp at Sheikh Nuran, in Palestine, at exactly the same time as a group of men and their camels had assembled for an inspection by the battalion's veterinary section. The attack resulted in the deaths of two men, with a further nineteen wounded.

The Commonwealth War Graves Commission website shows two men of the 3rd (Australian) Battalion, Imperial Camel Corps, who were killed on the same day, Tuesday, 5 June 1917. Trooper 2059 Victor Spinks, and 28-year-old Corporal 2363 Gerald Arthur Collett. They have no known grave, but their names are commemorated on the Jerusalem Memorial, on panels 59 and 60. Sadly, one can only assume that as they have no graves, they must have literally been blown to pieces in the subsequent explosion, which also killed twenty-six camels. A further fifteen had to be put down as a result of the injuries that they sustained in the attack.

Besides the Imperial Camel Corps there was also the Camel Transport Corps, which was a unit of the regular British Army, which had been formed in December 1915. It was not a fighting unit, and had never been intended for such use. The men who served in it were local Egyptian camel-handlers. It was a large unit with some 11,000 cameliers looking after 20,000 camels.

The corps played an important and vital role in keeping the troops on the ground supplied with all they required to do their job. The transport companies collected supplies directly from the ships and took them to the nearby waiting trains, which delivered them to the Imperial Camel Corps depot, thus ensuring that their troops never ran short of the equipment, food, water and ammunition they needed to take with them on their long distance patrol.

Camels were also used to ferry soldiers who had been wounded on the front line to hospitals in the rear. A contraption of bamboo was placed across the top of the camel, which allowed for two men to be carried in the prone position on either side.

The Camel Transport Corps was one of the auxiliary services that operated throughout Egypt. So effective were their members that they won 'golden laurels' for their devotion to duty on numerous occasions. Although they were a non-combatant corps, the exigencies of the advance across the desert, where camels are usually the only form of transport, meant that they and their riders were quite often in a position of risk and even grave danger. But despite this, the riders always displayed a splendid indifference to having been exposed in this manner, albeit unintentionally. When this occurred, the men behaved with great coolness and gallantry whilst under fire.

Camels carrying wounded soldiers through the dessert.

CAMELS

Men of the Camel Corps were recruited from a class inured to hardship, and were accustomed to facing long perilous journeys. This helped the men develop qualities of self-reliance, doggedness and the ability to endure. This resulted in the men of the Camel Corps receiving unstinted praise from their officers, and well-merited recognition from Higher Command, some even being recognised for their gallant conduct. Here are just a few examples of the men's personal bravery, whilst also highlighting the excellent endurance and bravery of the camels.

Bash Reis Abbas Said Mahmoud and Reis Mahommed Osman were in charge of a convoy of wounded in cacolets (a seat or bed fitted to a camel for carrying the sick or wounded) which they brought in safely under shell fire, whilst maintaining a cool attitude.

Driver Younis Gad, who had been wounded in the head, stuck to his camels, and did not report sick, until lines had been put down in a new camp, seven hours later. His injuries were found to be so serious that he had to have one of his eyes removed and a trepanning operation performed on his skull.

Another man named Reis took his camels to a dump 150 yards from the firing line and assisted the soldiers in carrying ammunition to the men in their trenches, who were at the time under attack from machine gun, rifle and shell fire.

During operations in April 1917, after a British ambulance was shelled, it was decided to remove everything and everybody to the rear. The Camel Transport Corps was called upon to assist, and rendered yeoman service. During the move, nineteen shells were fired at the camel convoy, all of which fell fairly close. Despite this, the drivers continued to lead their camels as if nothing out of the ordinary had happened.

At Duerdar, the men were ordered to remove a large number of camels behind a particular hill for safety. It was necessary to make a risky journey, not once, but on three separate occasions. Bash Reis Abdullah Kheri behaved splendidly all day, and led his men on all three occasions.

After the battles of Romani and Rafa, several men of the Camel Transport Corps were singled out for reward. When questioned as to what they would prefer, nearly all asked that it should be in the shape of money. Their wish was granted, although consideration was also given to provide them with a more permanent distinction to commemorate their actions. Some were bought watches which were inscribed with a record of their bravery.

Fifty-three camel drivers were on a sea journey when the steamer that they were travelling on was torpedoed by a German submarine. Five of the men were lost, whilst thirty-two were picked up by a Greek steamer and taken into Port Said in Egypt. The other sixteen had a most adventurous time, cast adrift from the others in a small boat during the course of the night.

Whilst the camel may well be the 'ship of the desert', a camel driver usually has as much notion of ordinary sea-going vessels as a rat-catcher has of whaling. None of the men had ever been to sea before. But despite this obvious handicap, they drifted in the Mediterranean for three-and-a-half days. Their boat even sprang a leak, but they didn't panic, they simply plugged it up the best that they could, and carried on their way. The men were picked up by a British warship and taken to Alexandria, feeling rightly proud of themselves. Despite their experience, twenty-two of the forty-eight survivors volunteered to undertake another similar journey. Having men with that type of 'can do' attitude, working with the camels, made for a very durable combination of man and beast.

Throughout March and April 1918, soldiers of the Arab Army defeated elements of the Turkish Camel Corps. On 16 March, a detachment of Sherif Abdulla's Army surprised a company of the Turkish Camel Corps near Jedahah, under cover of a sand storm. Thirty Turkish soldiers and fifty-five of their camels were killed, whilst the remainder fled in panic and disarray.

On 19 March, the Hedjaz Railway was attacked by a party of Sherif Ali's force near Bovat, with the result that some 3,000 rails, along with some culverts, were destroyed. Similar attacks continued across the region on 20, 23, and 24 March and 7 April.

In September 1918, C.G. Hurren wrote a letter to the editor of the *Bedfordshire Times and Independent* newspaper. Hurren had previously served with the cavalry, but said that given the choice between riding horses or camels, he preferred the ships of the desert. In his letter, he commented on the Imperial Camel Corps to which he belonged. He believed he was the only man from Bedfordshire who was a member of the corps and described its excellent work in the desert. As well as carrying out routine patrols, one particular stint saw Hurren's patrol spend three days and nights tracking across the desert, before going straight into action. Before the confrontation with the enemy, it had been raining continuously, and he described the sad figure of a camel in those circumstances, wallowing about on wet ground, feeling sorry for itself.

Hurren and his colleagues reached a stage where they had to dismount from their animals and operate as infantry soldiers because the camels' effectiveness amongst the hills was so greatly reduced.

The Memorial for the Imperial Camel Corps can be found in Victoria Gardens, on the Thames Embankment in central London. It was unveiled by Lieutenant General Sir Philip Chetwode in 1921, the same individual who had been the very first commander of the Desert Mounted Corps, of which the Imperial Camel Corps Brigade had been part.

Imperial Camel Corps Memorial.

The unveiling was a solemn occasion as was in keeping with such events. Guests included the Australian and New Zealand Prime Ministers of the day, Mr Billy Hughes and Mr William Massey. Also present were a number of cameliers who had served with the brigade during the war, along with Brigadier General Clement Smith who had been the brigade's commander throughout the war.

There are bronze plaques on the upper plinth, which include the names of those men who lost their lives during the First World War, whilst serving with the Imperial Camel Corps.

Chapter 9

Blue Cross

The Blue Cross charity was founded on 10 May 1897 in London, as *Our Dumb Friends League*, to care for sick and injured horses that were working on the streets of London, whose owners did not care for them properly. Horses were used by many, as either beasts to pull heavily laden wagons or as taxi cabs, but were often only seen as a means to an end for earning a living. When they were sick or injured they were more likely to be destroyed than receive veterinary attention.

Blue Cross poster.

The charity raised sufficient funds to open its first animal hospital in Victoria, London, on 15 May 1906, just nine years after it had been founded. It was a remarkable achievement and a mark of just how much British people loved their animals. In 1912, the league launched The Blue Cross Fund to care for horses during the Balkan War.

At the outbreak of the First World War in 1914, the Blue Cross Fund was quickly reopened, and by the signing of the Armistice in 1918, the Blue Cross Fund had raised nearly £170,000, the equivalent of almost £6.5 million today. All of this money went on care for the animals of conflict. The charity also offered its help to the British

War Office. This was politely turned down because the army had its own veterinary corps, which the War Office thought would be sufficient to deal with the number of horses that would need veterinary treatment. Maybe the authorities assumed that there wouldn't be a large number of wounded horses, believing there was more chance of horses being killed than there was of them being wounded.

But it was during the course of the First World War that the Blue Cross came into its own, when it ended up treating over 50,000 sick and injured horses and some 18,000 dogs in their hospitals spread out across the Western Front. Most of this work was funded by donations from the generosity of an animal-loving British public.

The charity also sent veterinary supplies to more than 3,500 units of the British and Allied armies, regardless of which theatre of war they were operating in, for the treatment of horses. Each of the supply packages sent by the Blue Cross contained drugs, bandages, horse salts and dressings, medicines, ointments, clippers, antiseptic, portable forges, and equipment for euthanising horses who were suffering and too badly wounded to recover.

Each ambulance that the Blue Cross sent out to the numerous different theatres of war cost £2,000, and despite the War Office declining their offer of help, on one occasion an impressed King George V was more than happy to inspect one of the fully equipped motor-horse ambulances in the grounds of Buckingham Palace. That must have made for an interesting topic of conversation when the king had his regular weekly meeting with his prime minister. The ambulance in question was on its way to Salonika, and the commander-in-chief of British Forces there sent his grateful thanks to the Blue Cross.

A representative from the Royal Society for the Prevention of Cruelty to Animals (RSPCA) wrote a letter to the editor of the *Scotsman* newspaper, which appeared in one of the December 1914 editions of the paper.

> Sir,
> I have much pleasure in commending to the generosity of all lovers of horses, the RSPCA fund for sick and wounded horses. We know how much they contribute to the efficiency of an Army, but we have comparatively little conception of the terrible suffering which modern warfare inflicts upon them.

The organisation of the Army Veterinary Department, with its fully equipped base and mobile hospitals and veterinary corps is, as has been recently testified in the Public press, as complete and efficient as human foresight and human skill can make it, but the growth of the work necessitates further machinery. The RSPCA fund established with the approval of the Army Council, and carried out under its direction and orders, is an auxiliary to supplement the work, including the training of competent assistants, the provision of motor lorries and ambulances, of medical and surgical stores and appliances, of rugs, of portable stoves for preparing food for the horses, and of anything and everything required for their care. To further such good and absolutely necessary work is the object of the RSPCA fund.

There are without doubt thousands of animal lovers who have desired to help our country's horses at the front. Equally so there must be thousands who desire to help towards the success of our arms by nursing the wounded horses back to health and efficiency. To you therefore, I would appeal for generous help.

Contributions should be forwarded to the Hon. Secretary, RSPCA. Fund for Sick and Wounded Horses, 105 Jermyn Street, London, SW, cheques to be crossed Messrs Coutts & Co.

Lady Olive Smith-Dorrien, who was the society's president, made an eloquent appeal for funds for the society, to an American audience, by way of a letter she wrote, and which was published by the editor of the *New York Times* newspaper, on 15 December 1915. She had actually written the letter on 11 October 1915. Before reading her words, it is worth remembering that not only did America not enter the war until 6 April 1917, it had never been a foregone conclusion that she would enter the war on the side of the Allies. One of the reasons being that she had a large German population, numbering nearly half-a-million people, with the majority coming from Chicago.

This great European war is, I am well aware, taxing the charitable and patriotic to the very utmost, but there is one especially worthy object which I submit should not be overlooked, and that is the alleviation of the sufferings of our horses. Without horses war could not be waged, this apart from the humane side of the question. The reduction of wastage among them must be a matter of great moment to the cause.

In 1912, 'Our Dumb Friends League' started a branch called the Blue Cross Fund, which aimed at the care of horses in war time. This organisation is now firmly established and has four large hospitals in France, which opened at the commencement of the war, and have not widened their field of action, but have increased in efficiency during the past year. These hospitals have received full recognition from the French Government, and our offers of help for French horses have been gratefully accepted and freely taken advantage of. Indeed some 2,000 wounded horses have been cured in our stables, the normal number of horses under our care being 600 or 700.

In addition to the care of animals, we have been able to supply large quantities of medicines, instruments, bandages, horse clothing, disinfectants, and fly nets, not only to mounted Corps of the regular British armies, but also to those raised for the help of the Empire by our great self-governing dominions, the commanding officers of many of which have written most gratifying letters of thanks and appreciation.

Over £3000 a month is needed to carry this work on its present scale, and up to date we have received this amount from our lovers of horses from all parts of the Empire. In view, however, of the extended duration of the war, the committee are naturally solicitous as to whether this flow of subscriptions can be maintained, and it is on this account I am making this further appeal for subscriptions, which may be sent addressed as follows:

Mrs Elphinstone Maitland, Honorary Secretary for United States of America, 829 Park Avenue, New York City.

Lady Smith-Dorrien, President Blue Cross Fund, 58 Victoria Street, London, SW.

Two things particularly stand out about the letter. Just how effective could the appeal possibly be, with America still another sixteen months away from entering the war, and a nation with a large German population? Secondly, and very noticeably, is the lack of endorsement by the British Government, despite France's enthusiasm and support for the society's continued level of committed work for the animals of the nation.

In March 1916, the Royal Society for the Prevention of Cruelty to Animals placed adverts in the press to inform the public of the work that the society had been carrying out, and how they could best assist.

> What the RSPCA fund is doing for the British Army Horses. It is working with the approval of the War Office, in conjunction with the Army Veterinary Corps, for the horses of the British Army, and it is the only fund that has been authorised for this purpose. It is supplementing the provision already made by the War Office, and is supplying motor lorries, horse ambulances, corn crushers, and chaff cutters driven by petrol engines, rugs, halters, bandages, and other veterinary requisites; it has provided Veterinary Hospitals to accommodate 3,500 horses, besides giving shelters to hold 500 horses.
>
> The RSPCA has in addition trained and sent to the British Army Veterinary Corps, for enlistment nearly 200 men, including many of the Society's own Inspectors, and is giving special lectures on the care and treatment of horses to NCOs and other soldiers. The RSPCA has also helped the British Army Horse at Home by supplying ambulances, rugs, humane killers, veterinary stores and medicaments to regiments all over the country. This has entailed a vast expense, which the generous public has helped the RSPCA to defray; but more aid will be required as the war continues.
>
> In the name of humanity, we beg you to send us a donation. Send it now to the Honorary Secretary, 105 Jermyn Street, London, SW.

The work undertaken by the RSPCA was invaluable and is to be highly commended, and without it, thousands of horses would have no doubt died. But it demonstrates how ill-prepared the War Office was at the start of the war, and how reliant they had to become on the RSPCA and the Blue Cross, when it came to the welfare and treatment of the horses that served in the British Army.

I personally find it almost unbelievable that those who worked in the War Office during the course of the First World War, and who one assumes were reasonably intelligent people, could get things so badly wrong. Surely there must have been at least one individual working in that department who had a modicum of intelligence, and some kind of military knowledge to recognise the number of horses that were going to be wounded and killed. It is not as if the war suddenly started without any warning, it was an inevitability that had been years in the making. It has got to go down in the history of mankind, as one of the worst kept secrets ever, and still the War Office miscalculated so badly, it's as if they didn't care. Remember if you will, this is the same War Office, and the same people, who when the Blue Cross Fund offered similar help and services to the RSPCA, were turned down and told that this aspect of the war had been sufficiently catered for. Really?

By April 1917, the Blue Cross and the RSPCA, whose funds had both been registered under the War Charities Act 1916, had been working together in France and had been directly responsible for opening ten complete animal hospitals across the Western Front. Collectively, the hospitals had treated a staggering 364,000 horses, of which 262,080 had recovered sufficiently to be returned to duty.

Saturday, 7 September 1917, saw the Blue Cross fete take place at Redhill sports ground in Surrey. Despite the fact that the event clashed with the Reigate Flag Day, the fete was very well supported, especially by those who had a love of everything to do with horses, and who truly had their welfare at heart.

To achieve such an attendance a varied and diverse programme had been arranged. Some of the events had a distinctly sporting theme about them, whilst others had a strong military element, both of which simply added to the atmosphere, and made for some keenly contested events. Others were of a more humorous nature, and provoked unrestrained merriment. These tended to be the events which had been set aside for the participation of wounded soldiers.

The day's most eagerly awaited event was without doubt, the Blue Cross Derby, which attracted a large and competitive field. The official starter was Captain Cecil Leveson Gower, who lowered the flag to get the runners and riders away on a circular three-lap course. The race was easily won by Mr H. Luscombe, with Mr Knapman securing second place, and Miss Davies finishing a very creditable third. After making a slow start, she didn't really get going until the beginning of the second lap, when she then proceeded to pass all of the other runners and just failed to catch Mr Knapman in second place. If the race had been just a few yards longer, she could have well caught him and reversed their positions. There was a similar race run over hurdles, which attracted a similar number of competitors and spectators, and was won comprehensively by Mr Samuel Marsh, with second place being secured by Lieutenant C.T.I. Roark, who was serving with the Life Guards.

There was also a show-jumping event, won by Mr Samuel Marsh, who additionally won a prize for best pony.

The day was a great success, with events catering for all the family, some being taken more seriously than others. The aim was to raise as much money as it could for the funds of the Blue Cross, which thankfully it did.

One of the ways that the Blue Cross attempted to raise funds was by writing letters to newspapers across the country, which they then published in one of their editions. In essence, the letters were asking people to donate to the charity, or to purchase their postcards and posters. One such letter appeared in the *Birmingham Daily Post* at the end of September 1917. It was written by the local branch Honorary Secretary, Mrs R. Blanckensee, who lived at 109 Harborne Road, Edgbaston.

> Sir,
>
> May I plead very earnestly with those who have subscribed so liberally to the many war charities, to spare yet something more for the horses which are taking so active a part in this terrible struggle?
>
> No one could possibly describe what war means to the horse, and especially such a war as this. The long winters of cold and mud, the torment of flies in summer, and the terror and fright of the battle followed by the agony of the bullet and shrapnel wounds, are but the fringe of the suffering a horse may endure.
>
> The Blue Cross has done much to relieve these sufferings, and it can still do more, provided the funds are maintained.

The Blue Cross helps the horses of all the Allies, and it also has a special service for wounded and sick dogs of war.

One of the Blue Cross Hospitals in France is called the Birmingham, and money from the Midlands is urgently needed for its maintenance. I should be most grateful to any ladies or gentlemen who will arrange to give sales of work, entertainments, collections, shop window displays of Blue Cross goods, or any other way of raising money for the Fund, and should be glad if they would communicate with me. Donations and subscriptions will be gratefully acknowledged by, Yours truly,

Mrs R. Blanckensee.

Throughout the war, Luton, and its people, were a town and a community that prided themselves on having raised funds for numerous different charities, which during the course of the First World War had been formed for the comfort of those who were engaged on the Allied side. In October 1917, the townspeople recognised that one such charity that they had not raised monies for was the Blue Cross Society. Not that they had any moral or legal duty to do so, they were simply a town who liked to give, and support worthy causes who were doing their bit for the war effort.

To rectify the matter a swimming gala was held at Luton's public baths on Monday, 8 October 1917, in an effort to raise much-needed funds for the society. There were animal hospitals already established in locations abroad, including France, Italy and Salonica, and the French government had appealed to the society to establish a fully equipped canine hospital in Paris, and to add kennels to each of the horse hospitals in France, where the *chiens de sante*, or dogs that had been used in the war as sentinels and to search for wounded soldiers, could also be treated by the veterinary surgeons.

The society had been able to undertake its work for more than three years because of the monies that had been raised, largely by public donations, but to be able to continue its work, and increase its output, it needed to continually raise funds, as it received absolutely no financial help from the War Office.

Lady Olive Smith-Dorrien, wife of General Sir Horace Lockwood Smith-Dorrien, who played such a prominent role in the vigorous and successful defensive action during the orderly retreat in the aftermath of the Battle of Mons, had the support as treasurer, of General Sir Leslie Rundle, GCB, who retired from the British Army in 1916, after having served for 40 years.

Together they made a formidable team. Their hands-on support most definitely helped the society in its fundraising initiatives.

The continuous good work of the Blue Cross was highlighted in a short letter sent by an officer who had served in the front line on the Western Front in France, to a friend of his in London.

> There is a fund called the Blue Cross, which is well worth your while to send a 'bob' to, as every little helps. It is for the benefit of sick and wounded horses. The poor dumb brutes suffer a lot in war time, and if you tell all your friends to send a little, you can assure them that they are doing good to those who cannot speak for themselves.

Painting entitled 'Goodbye Old Boy'.

Tuesday, 13 November 1917, saw a lecture given at the Queens, Birmingham, by Mrs Hatheway Turnbull, on the story of the Blue Cross and the part that animals were playing in the war. Sir Francis Lowe, the Member of Parliament for Birmingham Edgbaston, who chaired the meeting, emphasised the great importance of the work and the need for a continued effort to obtain funds, owing to the heavy drain that the war was having on the society's resources. Horses, he said, were just as likely to be struck by shells and bullets as soldiers were, and the Blue Cross Society had done some splendid work by establishing hospitals behind the lines in many parts of France, and by gathering in the horses who fell wounded on the field of battle.

Mrs Turnbull referred to the society's excellent work for the French and Belgian horses. Sadly, the Blue Cross was not supposed to help British horses, as the War Office had turned down their offer of help, believing they had sufficiently catered for this need with the Army Veterinary Corps. But they hadn't. That was not to say that the Army Veterinary Corps didn't do a fantastic job, because they did, but they didn't have sufficient surgeons and other personnel to deal with the unprecedented number of wounded horses. However, despite the War Office declining the help of the Blue Cross, the society had spent some £30,000 of its funds treating British horses.

Mrs Turnbull spoke of the kindness and consideration invariably displayed by the British 'Tommies' for their horses, and how their attitude was having a positive knock-on effect on nearly all Allied nations, in how they treated and cared for their animals.

Throughout 1917, there were numerous events across the United Kingdom, to raise much needed monies for the charity. It was as if every part of the country wanted to help add to the society's funds.

The Blue Cross Society continued its work into the Second World War, where because of charitable donations, it was able to offer veterinary care for more than 350,000 animals who were wounded during the aerial bombing of many of the nation's cities.

The name of the appeal fund became more widely known than the official charity title of *Our Dumb Friends League* and so it officially changed its name to *The Blue Cross* in 1950. In 2011 the charity dropped 'The' from its name and is now simply known as *Blue Cross*.

With the Armistice signed and the fighting finally at an end after four-and-a-half bloody years, the suffering and treatment of the wounded still continued, and for some it would continue for years to come. It was no different for the horses who had more than done their bit in the war effort. Just because the war was at an end, those animals who had been wounded still needed, care, love, affection, and maybe more.

Importantly, many of them still required veterinary treatment. Perhaps now the War Office would look to cover the cost of caring for the sick horses who had survived the war and been returned to the United Kingdom and finally take responsibility for the care and wellbeing of these fine animals. However, the government chose to allow a large number of horses be looked after by the goodwill and efforts of the same charitable organisations that had cared for them throughout the war.

By 16 November 1918, the RSPCA and the Blue Cross were still appealing for gifts and money to enable their outstanding work in caring for the sick and wounded horses who had served during the First World War to continue. The RSPCA aimed to raise £50,000, around £1,620,500 in current values. Although the work of the RSPCA and Blue Cross had saved the War Office considerable sums of money and some believed the government had a moral obligation to fund the care of the horses they had requisitioned, no public money was forthcoming.

Chapter 10

Animals in War Memorial

Despite animals having been used for military purpose during both the First and Second World Wars, a memorial to those who were killed or died whilst serving with British forces was only unveiled as recently as 24 December 2004, in Hyde Park, London, by Princess Anne, the Princess Royal. It was commissioned by the Imperial War Museum and designed by the English sculptor David Backhouse, and is made out of Portland stone.

The memorial came about as a result of public donations which ended up raising the staggering amount of £1.4 million. It includes the following inscriptions:

> This monument is dedicated to all the animals that served and died alongside British and allied forces in wars and campaigns throughout time.
>
> Many and various animals were employed to support British and Allied Forces in wars and campaigns over the

Animals in war, Memorial.

centuries, and as a result millions died. From the pigeon to the elephant, they all played a vital role in every region of the world in the cause of human freedom. Their contribution must never be forgotten.

Although the memorial is to commemorate all animals from across the centuries who have died whilst serving in the military forces of Great Britain, never was that more pronounced than during the four-and-a-half years of the First World War, where it is estimated that 8 million horses, mules and donkeys died, along with 100,000 pigeons.

Sources

www.k9history.com
www.cwgc.com
www.ancestry.co.uk
www.britishnewspaperarchive.co.uk
www.nzhostory.govt.nz
www.redcross.org
www.bluecross.org.uk
Wikipedia
www.museumof militarymedicines.org.uk
www.pigeoncontrolservicecentre.org

About the Authors

Stephen and Tanya Wynn have been together for the last fifteen years. Initially their shared interest was that of their four German Shepherd dogs, but when Stephen caught the writing bug in 2010, Tanya was a big influence on his first book: *Two Sons in a Warzone - Afghanistan: The True Story of a Father's Conflict*. Stephen kept a diary whilst his sons were both serving in Afghanistan during 2008. It remained a diary until Tanya persuaded him to turn it into a book. *Animals in the Great War* is the third book that they have written together, the first effort being *Women in the Great War* in 2017, and the second, *A History of the Royal Hospital Chelsea 1682-2017: The Warriors' Repose* in 2019. They now have another common interest.

When Stephen and Tanya are not busy writing, they can be found out walking their dogs early each morning when most sensible people are still fast asleep.

Index